SURREY

WALKS FOR MOTORISTS

W. A. Bagley

**Thirty sketch maps
by the author**

FREDERICK WARNE

FREDERICK WARNE
Penguin Books Ltd, Harmondsworth, Middlesex, England
Viking Penguin Inc., 40 West 23rd Street, New York, New York 10010, U.S.A.
Penguin Books Australia Ltd, Ringwood, Victoria, Australia
Penguin Books Canada Ltd, 2801 John Street, Markham, Ontario, Canada L3R 1B4
Penguin Books (N.Z.) Ltd, 182–190 Wairau Road, Auckland 10, New Zealand

First published as *London Countryside Walks for Motorists: South West* 1976
Second edition, under the title *Walks for Motorists: Surrey*, 1982
Reprinted with adaptations 1986

Publishers' Note

While every care has been taken in the compilation of this book, the publishers cannot accept responsibility for any inaccuracies. But things change: paths are sometimes diverted; concrete bridges replace wooden ones; stiles disappear. Please inform the publishers if you discover anything like this on your way.

The length of each walk in this book is given in miles and kilometres, but within the text Imperial measurements are quoted. It is useful to bear the following approximations in mind: 5 miles = 8 kilometres, ½ mile = 805 metres, 1 metre = 39.4 inches.

Made and printed in Great Britain by
Cox & Wyman, Reading

Contents

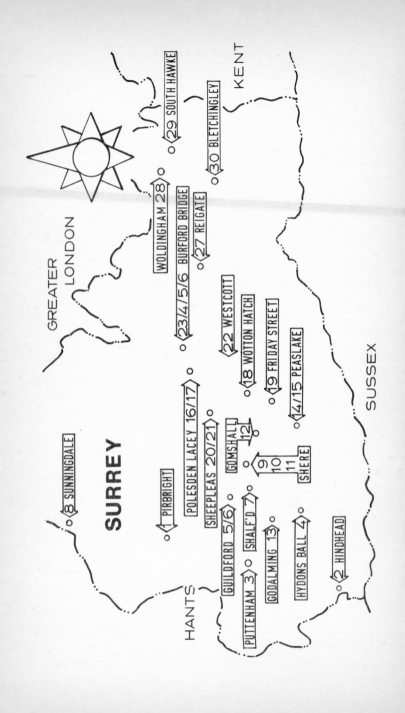

Introduction

More and more people are happily taking to country walking for recreation and Surrey has always been a favourite Home County for this purpose. This book, originally entitled *London Countryside Walks for Motorists: South Western Area,* contained walks based mainly in Surrey, with the exception of a few incursions into neighbouring Berkshire. It seems that most readers prefer walks books devoted to one county, so I have revised this edition substituting the old 'Berkshire' walks for new walks in Surrey.

In presenting these walks I have kept the 'occasional walker' in mind. As a countryside walker of long experience I know full well that the inexperienced rambler who blissfully believes that all public rights of way indicated on Ordnance Survey maps or on footpath signposts represent *walkable* paths is likely to run up against frustrations.

I have tried very hard to avoid these snags. Fortunately, in such a popular walking county as Surrey, with its wealth of commons, National Trust and Surrey County Council properties and Green Belt land, these hazards are, understandably, much fewer than in less visited areas. At the same time I would urge all who become keen on footpath conservation to join the Ramblers' Association (1/5 Wandsworth Road, London SW8 2LJ) and also to join their local Footpath Society or a rambling club and to go on some of their organized walks. These, almost invariably, aim to 'show the flag' over some of the more obscure and lesser-used paths which might otherwise die through lack of use. Very often footpath clearance parties are organized.

For the purpose of the present book, however, I have, often by two or three surveys for each walk, used only those paths over which, barring any completely unforeseen changes, you can reasonably expect enjoyable walking. There will be some, usually obvious, slight changes, of course, due to the effects of farm, forest, estate or other management or to latter-day building development, but the line of the right of way (as I describe it) should remain, unless it has been legally diverted. Such changes can usually be taken, metaphorically and literally, in one's stride. I have avoided routes which may be affected by proposed new roads. If the walker finds any significant changes, I would be very grateful to hear of them c/o the publisher.

My own maps have been specially drawn to indicate, boldly, the salient features of each route. Each will show, at a glance, far more place names than the necessarily brief contents list can. For extra detail and as a safeguard, especially if unforeseen circumstances compel a change of route, it is useful to carry an Ordnance Survey map. The 1:50,000 (2 cm to 1 km, or approx 1¼ in to the mile) serves very well and the sheet numbers of the appropriate maps are given at the beginning of each walk. Sheets 176 (West London), 186 (Aldershot and Guildford) and 187 (Dorking, Reigate and Crawley) cover all the walks in this book.

I have purposely avoided stating the open days and times of 'show' houses and gardens visited since these can vary from one season to another. At most public libraries, however, one can consult such booklets as the National Trust's guide and others covering houses and gardens open to the public.

Especially in woodland, please give every word of my description its full weight. If you should find that your surroundings do not tally with my description, go back to the last 'sure' place and try again. It could well be that, possibly aided by some trick of the lighting or conditions of foliage, some other beguiling path has seduced you from the one I describe. Never attempt to retrieve your position by taking short cuts over private land.

I have derived great pleasure from planning and doing these walks and I hope you get equal enjoyment. I wish you good walking and fine weather.

The following will help you to interpret the sketch maps:

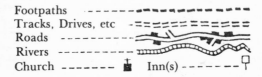

The inn symbol merely indicates that there is at least one inn in the town or village named. In the text the inns are named as locating points on the route.

Acknowledgements

For much-valued help with this book I should like to express my thanks to my brother, John, and to fellow members of the Vanguard Rambling Club: Les Douglas, Colin R. Hills, Ian Mitchell, Briar Reader and Geoffrey Stevenson. And Kate, who contributed her four legs to my two, must also be mentioned as a tireless, good companion.

Walk 1

Shalford, St Martha's and The North Downs Way

8 miles (13 km)

OS sheet 186

The walk starts from the Seahorse at Shalford on the A281 just south of Guildford.

There is somewhat limited parking by the main road. Pub parking is quite possible but strictly with permission. As this is a circular route however, it may be based on the car park on Halfpenny Lane just below Tyting Farm. This can be reached by branching northwards off the A248 at Chilworth.

At the very start of the walk we pass the eighteenth century Shalford Mill on the Tilling Bourne which was grinding corn up to 1914. It later fell into decay and to save it from demolition a group of conservationists — 'Erb the Smasher', 'Bill Stickers', 'Black Mary' and others who comprised the anonymous 'Ferguson's Gang' — raised the money for repair and endowment and in 1932 handed the mill over to the National Trust. The mill, with most of its machinery and storage bins remaining, is open to the public. Consult the National Trust handbook for times of opening.

Chilworth Manor with its ancient fishponds and a Queen Anne walled garden is shown to the public on several occasions during the summer. (Consult National Gardens Scheme leaflets and handbook for details.)

The famous St Martha's Church we reach on this round is mainly a restoration of 1849 but the foundations of the hilltop church above Chilworth date from at least the late twelfth century and it is highly likely that the Christian church was built on a site where pagan rites were practised.

The Pilgrims' Way is met with in this and other walks in this book. The once-popular notion, fostered by romantic 'research' and apparent sponsorship by the Ordnance Survey, that this was a major route pioneered by medieval pilgrims travelling from Winchester to Canterbury to visit the shrine of St Thomas à Becket after his murder in 1170, finds much less support nowadays. What *does* seem undoubtedly true is that whether or not pilgrims later came this way, the present so-called Pilgrims' Way follows more or less a very ancient east-west trackway.

The North Downs Way, also met with in this and other walks in this book, is one of Britain's long-distance footpaths running some 150 miles, as the name implies, along the North Downs from

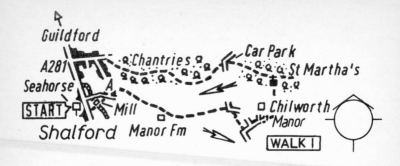

Farnham to Dover. It was first suggested by the Ramblers' Association and after a great deal of negotiation and striving for official
recognition (since some new paths were needed to link up with
existing rights of way—indeed, some extensions are still hoped for
and slight modifications may still be needed) it was officially opened
on 30 September 1978 by the then Archbishop of Canterbury, Dr
Donald Coggan.

Start the walk opposite the Seahorse and go down a paved path
signposted for Shalford Mill. The mill is passed on your left after
which you cross a stile and keep on by the left-hand side of a field.
Then cross another stile and go down steps on to a lane (point A).
Footpath stalwarts, anxious to 'show the flag', may go down the track
opposite only to find that it soon narrows and becomes enclosed
between hedges and soon so overgrown that one is compelled to go
through a left-hand gap and continue (forward) in the parallel lane.
Others may get on the metalled lane from the start.

Either way, in a couple of hundred yards from point A go
through a gap in the right-hand hedge to a stile. The ensuing field-
side path runs with a fence on your right. Cross another stile and,
disregarding another stile on the right, continue forward subsequently to cross a third stile, now bearing half right with the
hedge. At the next stile, at Manor Farm, you join a track.

Turn left and follow the sandy way between fields for just over
½ mile to reach a gate which gives exit to a road (Halfpenny Lane).
Turn rightwards in this for only a dozen yards or so and then, by a
house named 'Longmead' and at a 'No Horses' sign turn rightwards,
downhill, on a footpath. At its end, in a short ¼ mile, turn left to a
road elbow on the outskirts of Chilworth. Keep ahead and when the
road soon bends left, keep ahead on a drive by which, later bending
left, you reach the front of Chilworth Manor.

Pass in front of the manor and then, by a signposted footpath
turn left to pass the side of the house on your left and continuing
steeply uphill through trees and later over the transverse North

Downs Way to reach St Martha's.

There are seats on the south side from which you can admire the view which includes Albury Park, Hurt Wood, Blackheath and the Hascombe ridges. From the church proceed in a westerly direction (ie leftwards from your original uphill approach), descending the pine-clad slope, finally through an open area (ignoring a right-hand fork to the car park — unless, of course, you have parked there) out, via a sandy gulley to a road (Halfpenny Lane again).

Turn left, downhill for a short 50 yards and then turn rightwards. Keep *forward* through the woods (here, Farthing Copse) for about 25 yards and then, through the barrier, follow the main track through the woods bending half left soon to pass the wooden buildings of Youth Camp Site on your left, so to a stile. The way now runs finely along the top of hillside, open on the left and with Chantry Woods on your right. In about ¼ mile from the camp site, and at the second stile you meet, and at a red-painted Nature Trail post (one hopes that it has not been vandalized) get over a stile and turn half right following a wide footpath. Like other paths in the Chantry Woods area, this is not a public right of way but an amenity access path over an open area. Turn left on a transverse path and follow this out, soon downhill, later veering left to the valley bottom and to the white Chantry Cottage. Go forward through a gate (the western entrance to Chantry Woods) and come out on a road (the Pilgrims' Way). Follow it leftwards. It *can* be followed for about ¾ mile to the A281 where you turn left back to your starting point. But if a residential road is considered preferable to a main road just turn left in the first road after leaving Chantry Cottage. When you get near the end of this you will recognize that 'this is where we came in' and either retrace a little of your outward way via Shalford Mill or else turn rightwards on the transverse road out to the A281.

Walk 2   Hindhead Common and Thursley

7 miles (11 km)

OS sheet 186

The prime interest of this walk is Hindhead Common with, from Gibbet Hill, one of the widest views in southern England and the famous Devil's Punch Bowl.

Our ancestors seem to have had, topographically, a simple way of dealing with mounds and hollows. If they were fairly obviously man-made, ancient defence works and the like, they were credited to Caesar. But if they were due to some upheaval of nature they were attributed to the Devil.

Modern geologists tell us that the formation of the Devil's Punch Bowl, more formally Highcombe Bottom, is due to the fact that a number of streams have eroded the sand until a clay bottom was reached.

The wooded bowl, heather and bracken grown, did on one occasion actually run red. On 24 September, 1786, a sailor—his name has remained unknown—was apparently returning to his ship at Portsmouth and—most unusual in such circumstances—was well in funds. At Esher he had fallen in with three vagrants and had generously treated them to food and drink. The foursome then travelled together taking, via Thursley, the old coach road round the rim of the Punch Bowl. At this lovely spot the cupidity of the three hoodlums could be restrained no longer. They murdered the unfortunate mariner and after stripping him tossed his body casually into the Punch Bowl and nonchalantly continued their way. They must have been as stupid as they were vicious.

A couple of labourers passing that way soon afterwards (at first mistaking the naked human body for a sheep) discovered the murder and a hue and cry was raised. The three thugs were arrested that very evening near Petersfield whilst they were trying to sell their victim's clothes. They were convicted at Kingston Assizes and, on 7 April, 1787, hung in chains on a gibbet at the highest point of Hindhead Common, there to dangle and moulder for many years.

On this present walk you can see the site of the murder and after going along Sailor's Lane see the sailor's tombstone with its crude carving and tear-jerking ballad-style epitaph in Thursley churchyard.

Gibbet Hill (895 ft) is the second highest hill in Surrey (see Walk 14). In planning this route, a little main-road walking was found

12

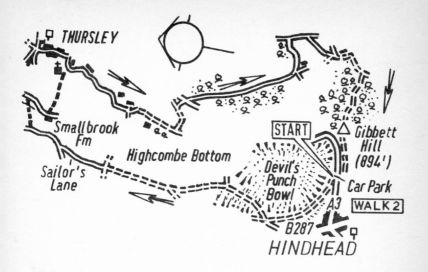

necessary in order to link up the otherwise 'green' ways—quite hilly in parts.

To arrive at the starting place take the Portsmouth Road (A3), via Guildford. Just before it crosses the Chichester-Farnham Road (A287) you will find the National Trust car park (free).

From the car park at Hindhead go over the grass between some posts, signposted 'Nature Trail', towards the view of the Devil's Punch Bowl. Turn left past a telescope and, with the Punch Bowl on your right, follow the waymarked path to a clear crossing track. Turn left along this and follow gently downhill to another track coming in from the left. Here bear rightwards passing a National Trust 'Highcombe' sign and follow this broad track downhill ignoring lesser tracks to left and right for about 1¼ miles.

The track narrows near the end and runs between banks to pass a metal gate and come out to a road at a corner. Here go straight ahead along Sailor's Lane and at the next road junction go right-wards, signposted to Elstead, and continue until reaching a sign-posted footpath on the right.

Follow this path gradually downhill crossing a small stream by a footbridge and out to a metalled track. Turn rightwards along this and follow its curves until you come to a stile on the left almost opposite Smallbrook Farm. Go over this stile and proceed half right over the following field to a stile in the far right corner. Then continue ahead with a line of trees to your left over a stile and then over another field and out to the churchyard at Thursley.

13

Just before the church, a little to your left, is the tombstone to the murdered sailor. The sordid story associated with this grave is softened by the beautiful view over to the Hogs Back.

Follow the path out through the churchyard to the road. Turn rightwards and follow this road for about ¾ mile. Just after passing Lower Highfield Farm take the track to the left and follow uphill until coming to a fork. Here go leftwards and follow this track out to a main road (A3).

Cross this to the road opposite, signposted to Brook, and follow this road round bends for almost a mile until you reach a transverse road. Here turn rightwards to, soon, a road on the right, signposted 'High Button'. Take this for a short distance to a track marked Polana Farm, on the right. Where this soon bends rightwards into private land, go straight ahead between hedges.

On coming to a junction of tracks just before a house, go straight ahead along that passing the house and then uphill through the trees ignoring crossing paths. This is quite a long steep hill! Take your time!

Continue around some twists and turns until meeting a junction of about seven tracks. Here take the path running uphill half right (just to the right of a tree marked 5). A little further and you are at the summit of Gibbet Hill.

Now turn left over the grass to join the tarmac track back into Hindhead noting on the right a stone memorial at the scene of the sailor's murder. Thus you return to the car park.

Walk 3

Puttenham, Puttenham Heath and Lydling Farm

5½ miles (9 km)

OS sheet 186

Puttenham is an attractive village lying under the Hogs Back and mostly strung along its one long street (part of the reputed Pilgrims' Way). Since parts of the Pilgrims' Way feature in other walks in this present book, a few brief notes may be of interest.

Until comparatively recently the accepted belief has been that after the murder of Thomas à Becket in 1170 his shrine in Canterbury Cathedral quickly became a place of popular pilgrimage. For reasons I have never found completely convincing, even when explained by such intellectuals as Hilaire Belloc in his famous *The Old Road* (1904), Winchester became a rallying point. From here the Pilgrims allegedly wended their way eastwards to Canterbury taking the most suitable of already-existing ancient tracks and merging them to form a more or less well-defined continuous Pilgrims' Way. (Note that Chaucer and Co. used a different route — along the Watling Street.)

The serious topographical researcher cannot, however, be an old-time romantic at the expense of latter-day questionings. Even those who originally wrote up the traditional belief (for example Eric Parker in his still much-loved *Highways and Byways In Surrey* (*1908*) have later (see the same author's *Surrey* in the Country Books series 1947) had to revise their thinking. It is pointed out that the earliest known record of the name Pilgrims' Way was in 1769 and no evidence has ever been adduced to the use of the Way by medieval pilgrims travelling regularly from Winchester to Canterbury. To us, as Pilgrims in quest of good country walking, does it really matter? By any other name . . .

As just noted, the Pilgrims' Way is made up of sections of ancient trackways. In places this has become a metalled, modern motorable road. In other places it has been relegated to Division Four or lower so far as present-day wheeled traffic is concerned. But it was once part of our early road system. The old trackways were, in their time, as important as the M-roads of today. Quiet today, they were once well used. Plenty of Pilgrims must have come this way together with packhorse proprietors, princes on palfreys along with their pages, perspiring priests and peripatetic parsons, palmers in procession, poachers and pot wallopers, plodding peasants . . . a varied host of pedestrians prehistoric, past and, now, present; a goodly company to

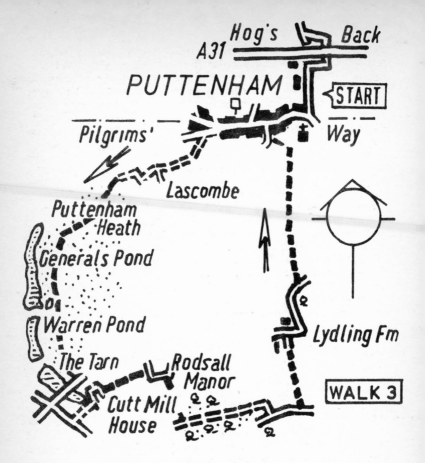

follow. So let us take the Pilgrims' Way in this spirit. We are in this present book concerned with the outdoor scene, not the scholars' library.

On a more material matter, note that Puttenham Heath, not too far from the start, makes a fine spot for a picnic meal.

Puttenham lies just south of the A31, west of Guildford. Discreet parking in the village should not be difficult.

From Puttenham take the Seale and Farnham Road (The Street) westward to where the road forks. Here go straight ahead up Lascombe Lane and at the fork keep left along Highfield Lane. Continue along this and at the junction of tracks take the one straight ahead signposted to Lascombe Farm and Sylvan Lodge. After a few yards, at another junction of tracks, continue straight ahead and at the end of farm buildings continue along the path ahead running between trees, through a gate and out to a T-junction of paths. Here turn rightwards and at the fork a few yards later bear left and a few yards later at a crossing track turn left.

Follow this grassy track around a number of twists and turns for about a ¼ mile until reaching a clear crossing track. Turn rightwards on this and head towards the trees, ignoring crossing paths. On reaching the trees turn left along a track with the trees behind a wire fence to your right. You will shortly pass the General's Pond and come to a fork.

Take the path to the right and follow to the edge of the quite beautiful Tarn. Continue ahead with the Tarn on your right. This includes a short diversion over a series of sleepers thoughtfully provided to save us getting too muddy. Follow this path out to a road on which turn rightwards until reaching a crossroads.

Turn left here by the signpost for Shackleford and Godalming and follow the road until soon coming to a clear track on the left by a public footpath sign. Go through the gate and follow the track to a sharp right corner. Here go over left and follow the path keeping the lake to your left. Just before a lakeside building on your left, turn right on to the drive and follow this right past a 'Tradesmen's Entrance' sign. At the end of the buildings on the right follow the road round to the right and continue until just after passing a house on your right. Follow a path between trees to a road at a corner.

Continue along the road for a few yards then bear right (with a hedge on your right) along a track and continue along this ignoring a fork to the right until meeting a crossing track.

Here turn left and continue up the soft track keeping straight ahead at junctions to a T-junction of tracks with a stile ahead. Cross the stile and go half right over the field to a stile almost at the far right-hand corner. Cross this, follow down to the road and continue your direction along the road to a signposted path on your left just before a house. Go along this keeping to the right-hand edge of a long field, at first with a garden hedge to your right and then beside wooden fencing. At the end of the first field on the right go through a gap and maintain your direction this time along, at first, the left edge of a field and then between fields towards a row of houses.

From here continue straight ahead along a broad track and bear right when this joins another track, pass Lydling Farm and continue out to a road. Turn left on this and after about a ¼ mile go left to a gate and stile by a public footpath sign. Follow this path at first running parallel to a hedge on the left then uphill with a barbed wire fence to the left, ignoring a wooden swing gate, to a stile on your left almost hidden by trees. Continue again half right over the field to a squeeze gap just to the right of a gate.

Go through this and follow the left edge of the field with a fence to your left to a stile by trees ahead. Cross this and go along the enclosed path over another stile. The path then bears left, crosses another stile and follows the right edge of a field out to a road (Suffield Lane) at Puttenham.

17

Since there is so much one can say about Compton, I must, since this is not a formal guide book, take refuge in saying but little except that Compton's Norman church is reputedly the most interesting in Surrey, and one of the finest in England. One can obtain, in the church, either a leaflet or a more detailed booklet describing the many unique features — the chapel built directly over the sanctuary, the Norman screen which is probably the oldest woodwork in England, and many other treasures.

G. F. Watts, the Pre-Raphaelite painter and sculptor lived in the village until his death in 1904. The Watts Picture Gallery, passed on this walk and which can be visited, contains a representative selection of his works.

On this round we get a mid-distance view of the mellow grey stone frontage of Loseley House, one of the most charming Elizabethan mansions in Surrey.

Guildford (usually pronounced Guil'f'd) hardly requires any 'finding'. There are several public car parks in Guildford including a multi-storey one (consult your Motoring Organisation's handbook). On Saturdays these car parks are apt to be crowded out and there is a time limit (which might well — as with street parking — be relaxed on Sundays). The railway station car park has no time limit. As this walk, like all the others in this book is circular, one may well consider parking discreetly at, say, Compton or Littleton and starting the walk there.

Although the Wey stretch is delightful, it can be omitted, especially if you decide not to park at Guildford centre. This walk can be regarded as being based on the Ship inn a short mile south of Guildford centre, on the A3100. Join the ramble by going up Sandy Lane opposite. Since you may be using any of the several car parks in Guildford, this walk is described as starting from the theatre — at the corner of Mill Mead at the western, lower, end of the famous High Street.

By the side of the theatre take the little short lane to Mill Mead Lock — often a scene of great animation. Proceed with the Wey on your left, soon passing a National Trust sign indicating that this is the Godalming Navigation.

May I say in parenthesis that the towpath can be followed all the

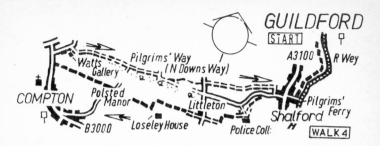

way to Godalming (about 4 miles) and a very nice walk it is, especially in lazy summer weather. The only technical snag from the point of view of this present book is that such a walk would not be circular though there is no lack of public transport back to Guildford. It is therefore offered as a suggestion only.

On the present walk we soon find, with the well-sited Jolly Farmer on the opposite bank, a footpath cutting off a bend of the river. The towpath is then rejoined. In about ¾ mile from Mill Mead Lock you come to the site of the so-called Pilgrims' Ferry (inoperative nowadays). This spot is easily recognized since it comes just before what, at first glance, appears to be a mini landslip of yellow-orange sand. There are paving slabs on the towpath and a lifebuoy hung up on a board. There is also what, again at first sight, appears to be a bit of 'Gothick' garden ornament — a little stone arch spanning a rivulet. It is, I believe, part of a tiny now-ruined chapel.

Turn in rightwards here, the path soon becoming a little lane. This is quite steep but short and brings you out, over the railway, to the main road. Here turn rightwards but very soon, opposite the Ship, go left in Sandy Lane. Keep to the left-hand side and where the sidewalk ends, as the road bends slightly rightwards, continue by a clear path, rising between banks. It runs to the side and at a higher level of the road you have just quitted.

The path then drops down to a drive. Cross this and keep ahead passing garages on your left and 'The Firs' nameplate on your right. Then, with a lamp post at the corner you continue by a track which soon becomes an enclosed path, with lovely views ahead.

On coming to a sandy cross track turn rightwards (with the electricity line). The track subsequently becomes a 'made' lane and brings you to a transverse road (at Littleton). Cross over passing a lovely half-timbered house on your right and the Youth House on the left.

From the white-painted metal field gate ahead continue over a large meadow to another gate and stile. Continue to another stile and over this keep forward in a track with the pond, which has been seen prominently ahead, on your left and Loseley House not far off.

19

Maintain your direction, wire fence on left, to white-painted metal field gates ahead. You cross a track here, not by getting over the gates but by using the stiles adjacent. Continue ahead but in only 20 yards or so, turn squarely left, now on the left-hand edge of a cropped field. Quite soon get over a stile on the left and at once resume your forward way, now by an enclosed path passing some fine old trees.

Thus you come to a stile with a privately-erected signpost. Here turn rightwards on a chestnut drive. You subsequently pass a lodge and continue out to a drive end at Polsted Manor. Now turn left and follow the quiet little lane out, disregarding a left-hand fork, to the B3000 where continue forward through Compton, passing the Harrow to reach the church on the left.

After looking round continue in the road, passing a half-timbered old house that was once an inn. Just before reaching the by-pass turn rightwards on the cul-de-sac road signposted for the Watts Galleries. Immediately before these Galleries turn rightwards on a hedged track. It is part of the ancient trackway now known as the Pilgrims' Way—see notes to Walk 3—and, hereabouts, forms a long-distance walking route, the North Downs Way. We meet it again in other walks in this present book.

Just keep ahead. The track rises and falls, rises and falls again. At times it runs between hedges and, through breaks to the left, you see the swell of the Hogs Back. At other times it runs, well wooded, between sandbanks. Disregard a transverse path.

In about a mile from Compton you will notice, by the side of the track, white gates of a type you saw on the earlier part of the walk. A little beyond these there is a left-hand turn running to a farm. Ignore this. Your way is ahead but note that you have, immediately, a choice of ways. (1) Take the undulating 'hollow way' track which runs just *inside* the woodland. This is a public bridlepath and part of the North Downs Way. It brings you out eventually to a road junction of Sandy Lane and Littleton Lane, looking very much like a bend of a fairground helter-skelter. Unless you care to presume on permission and turn squarely leftwards for about 250 yards to a farm road on the right, keep ahead in Sandy Lane—moderately residential but quite pleasant (and downhill!)— out to the main road at the Ship. (2) Keep forward along the *outside* of the woodland on a very clear track but in only 300 yards fork off half left and quickly resume your forward way, now not quite 100 yards from the track you have just quitted. You soon encounter an arm of woodland and the track subsequently runs out to a little lane. Cross to the rough farm road opposite and follow it out, finally round a right bend into Sandy Lane in which turn left to the main road at the Ship.

Now, for decided preference, retrace a little of your outward way back to Guildford. But if the shades of night are falling fast you could turn left in the main road for just under a mile.

Walk 5 Winkworth Arboretum and
Hydons Ball

6 miles (9.5 km)

OS sheets 186/187

The walk passes through the National Trust's Winkworth Arboretum, a hillside planted with rare trees and shrubs. There are fine views and it is well worth detouring, temporarily, from the basic route, for example down to the Lakes.

The Arboretum is open (free) until dusk all the year round. The best times to visit, if you have a choice in the matter, are probably April and the end of October.

Hambledon Church, separated ¾ mile from the village, was rebuilt in 1846, but parts date from the fourteenth century. As with Thursley (see Walk 2) there is a fine view from the churchyard over to the Hogs Back.

From the churchyard we ascend eastwards to Hydons Ball (593 ft) the top of which, and some 125 acres of the surrounding Heath was acquired as a memorial to Octavia Hill (1838-1919) the social reformer and one of the founders of the National Trust.

Pay careful attention to your usual road maps and to my own sketch map. From Godalming (on the A3100) branch off on the B2130 but in only a mile or so, after a square left-right turn, take the rightmost fork at a church. Very soon disregard a right and left fork. In a further mile or so, fork leftwards, through woodland. At the transverse lane then reached you will find, opposite, the National Trust's free car park (for Hydons Ball).

From the car park specified return to the road and turn rightwards (towards Hascombe). Follow the road for a ¼ mile until just before the road begins to descend fairly steeply, turn sharp left to a track. This narrows to a path in which continue at first with a wire fence on the right and then slightly leftwards past a wooden post and then through woodland.

At a junction where a path comes in on the right continue straight ahead through a gate. A track then comes in from the left. After a few more yards take the track bearing off uphill to the right. Follow this track. Just after 'The Cottage' it becomes metalled. Continue ahead to a road corner. Here turn rightwards and on coming to a main crossing road (the B2130) cross to the entrance to Winkworth Arboretum opposite.

Take the main broad track to the left of Fox Cottage and

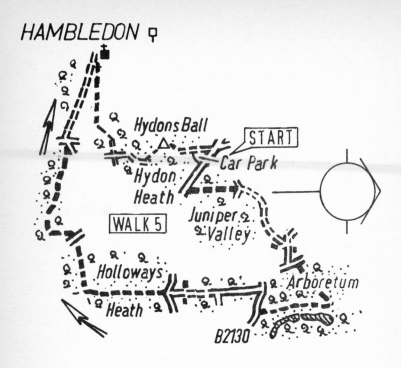

HAMBLEDON

Hydons Ball

START

Car Park

Hydon Heath

Juniper Valley

WALK 5

Holloways Heath

Arboretum

B2130

continue ahead, downhill, until you come to a fork. Here go to the right and follow this delightful path with the valley and lakes to the left. Where the path bends left by a bench (with trees ahead) turn rightwards and on reaching a wire garden fence ahead turn left and follow this path out to a road, in which turn rightwards.

At the next corner turn left to a metalled lane signposted to Hascombe Court. Follow this lane for about ½ mile, ignoring turnings to left and right, to a metalled crossing road. Cross this to the track opposite and follow this. After passing tracks to left and right, just after entering a wooded area, a clear crossing track is reached. Turn rightwards along this and at a fork bear right, downhill and out to a road near a bend.

Turn rightwards in the road for a few yards to a signposted bridleway on the left. This is the left of the two tracks running uphill to a wooden swing gate at the top on the right. Go through this and then along the left edge of the next two fields to another wooden swing gate at the far left corner. Go through this and resume your forward direction along the narrow path which wanders a little but stays not far from the top of the hillside.

22

Eventually you will come to a track coming in from the left. Here go rightwards for a few yards and then continue again in the forward direction with a field behind the fence to the right. This path soon joins a track and after a few more yards, just before Maple Bungalow on the right, turn sharp left to an enclosed sandy path. Continue ahead along this path until reaching the church at Hambledon.

On reaching the church turn sharp right on to the track coming in on the right. Note here the ancient lime kiln on the right. Pass now through a swing gate and continue straight ahead in line with the churchyard wall over a field to another swing gate. Go half left over the next field to a metal swing gate in its far corner, to the left of a wider farm gate. Pass through this and after a few yards bear right onto a sandy track and follow this until reaching a junction of tracks. Here take the one ahead following your forward direction through woodland and uphill.

Follow this track until coming to the second path leading off to the left just before a clearing on the right. Take this path and at a fork keep right and continue uphill, the path getting narrower as you climb, until coming up to the triangulation pillar at the summit of Hydons Ball, 593 ft. The stone seat in front provides a handy resting place to recover from the ascent.

From here take the track immediately behind the seat downhill to a broad crossing track. Turn left on this and follow out to the car park.

Walk 6

Guildford, Walnut Tree Bottom and St Martha's

6 miles (9.5 km)

OS sheets 186/187

This walk can be shortened to 4 miles (6.5 km) by starting at St Martha's.

Despite inevitable modernization, Guildford's steep High Street remains one of the most charming in Surrey. It is on this that we base the present (full) walk. The route, however, is Q-shaped and by using the car park west of St Martha's we cut off the tail of the Q and much of the subtopian aspect of the initial part of the main walk.

No motorist needs telling how to get to Guildford — the focal point of many roads. There are several parking places to choose from in Guildford, but all are likely to be heavily used on Saturday. For the St Martha's car park, branch off rightwards from the A246 at Chilworth. Go through the village and then round four square bends. Just after going through a gully you come to the car park on the right.

At Guildford go up the High Street and just before reaching the famous cantilevered clock on the left turn in rightwards through Tunsgate arch. Cross the transverse road that immediately follows and quite soon after this turn left to go up — steeply at first — Pewley Hill.

After nearly ½ mile the road ends and you continue forward on a wide grassy track along the breezy top of Pewley Down (hedge on your left). The small light-grey stone pillar over to your right is a viewfinder and you may well detour to inspect it and its inscription, though, nowadays, the view to the west and to the north is somewhat subtopian.

Resume, however, your original forward way. Just after passing abreast of the viewfinder ignore a path on the left but just after this (a couple of hundred yards past the viewfinder) branch off leftwards through a hedge gap and go at first by a field-edge footpath and then on to Warren Farm. Here turn left on the concreted drive out to the transverse Warren Road, in which turn rightwards. Where, in a couple of hundred yards, this bends rightwards, slant half left initially over a grassy triangle on a track which later acquires a surfacing. It then crosses a grassy open space and you pass a car park on the right to come to a T-junction.

Here turn squarely right on a stony track to pass the golf club-house on your left. In less than 100 yards past this slant off half left on a track over the Merrow Downs Golf Course. In ½ mile from the clubhouse you pass, in Walnut Tree Bottom, a white house with a brick and flint wall — a good example of the use of local materials in building.

In about 150 yards past this house, and just after the start of a clearing on the right, turn rightwards, uphill, on a narrow path, through the trees (The Roughs) going over crossing tracks to reach, through wooden barriers, a small car park. Turn left through the car park for a few yards and then go rightwards, downhill, on a path through the right-hand scrub. In 100 yards or so turn sharply right, downhill through trees, soon forking left to reach a road (White Lane) just short of a sharp bend.

Cross the road and go up steps opposite. You are now, as the signs indicate, on the North Downs Way. Turn left and follow the path (parallel to the road on your left) downhill. In a couple of hundred yards or so, just as the road on your left bears half left, veer half right to pass a cottage named 'Ramshackle' on your right.

You are now on a sandy track which is followed (rightwards at a fork) to the top of St Martha's Hill. St Martha's church is passed on your left and you continue, now downhill on the broad track, through pines. There is finally an open area on the right. Where this ends, and where the track bends rightwards to a car park, *keep ahead* on a footpath, soon through a sandy gully and out to a road (Halfpenny Lane).

Here turn rightwards, uphill for ¼ mile to cross tracks at Tyting Farm. Here turn leftwards. In ¼ mile (where you meet Chantry Woods) branch off half right on a track.

In due course you will find that 'this is where we came in' and so retrace your steps (fortuitously downhill) back to your starting point.

25

Walk 7 — Pirbright, Cobbett Hill and Bullswater Common

7½ miles (12 km)

OS sheet 186

Pirbright is a name often associated with the army, but the military barracks of Pirbright and Bisley are situated a mile away north-west from Pirbright *village* on which this ramble is based, and the present walk is mainly over the commons on the fringe of the army ranges to the south-west of the village.

As explorers ourselves, albeit gentle followers of the footpath way, we may note in Pirbright churchyard a huge block of unhewn Dartmoor granite marking the grave of Henry Morton 'Doctor Livingstone, I presume' Stanley.

In these days of (generally) metal footpath signposts, the number of *wooden* signposts currently in this area will be noted.

Pirbright village is easily located as it is on the A324. Park discreetly in the village. The best place if not already occupied is probably in the small layby by the village pond opposite the post office. (Turn off the A324 at the White Hart.)

Go eastwards along the road passing the village pond on your left and the Cricketers on your right and in 250 yards pass Chapel Lane on the right. About 100 yards further on (just past the 'Pirbright' roadsign) turn left on a bridleway, currently indicated by an elderly wooden signpost between pine trees. After nearly 200 yards cross a small plank bridge over a ditch; bear left over a second little bridge and then go forward through a clump of pines. In a further 50 yards cross a third plank bridge. Follow the path, swinging first left over yet another bridge (houses can be seen through the trees on your right) and then right to emerge on a little road.

Continue straight over as indicated by the wooden footpath sign, with iron railings on your right and between two houses. Here keep *forward* between gorse bushes, ignoring the clear track diverging left. Follow this narrow path up to the main road (A324) at an old-fashioned, green-painted lamp standard by a large sign. Cross the road and go along the track opposite, passing two houses and a bungalow on the right and so between concrete posts to reach a cross track. At the foot of the holly hedge on the left corner ahead is a concrete marker post bearing the inscription WD 1186 with an arrow between the letters. This marks the old boundary of the army lands and a number of such stones will be seen on this present ramble. As

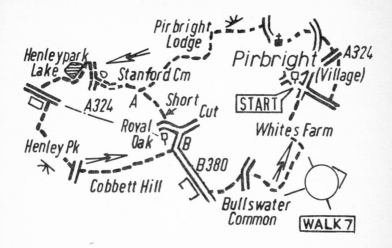

they are individually numbered, they are useful guides to use to describe the route, and numbers used later on in the text will refer to such stones.

Keep straight over the cross track, with the holly hedge on your left, to emerge on an estate road. Turn left for 50 yards to reach the B3405 in which turn right. In a further 50 yards or so turn left (no signpost here) between holly hedges on a clear track. You will soon see Pirbright church ahead—our next objective. The track narrows after 150 yards, past a sign 'Footpath Only, No Horses'. Keep forward on this clear path which will bring you to the church on your left after ¼ mile.

Turn half right along the lane and follow it round a right bend, ignoring a footpath on the left. About 50 yards *after* passing 'Apple Tree Cottage' on the left, turn left (wooden footpath sign) between barbed wire fences and soon cross a substantial plank bridge with an iron handrail. The path curves left to a stile in the right-hand fence; cross this and immediately turn squarely right across a field, heading for the left edge of a clump of trees. On reaching the clump, keep slightly left and uphill, with a barbed wire fence on your right and gorse bushes left, to reach a stile (there are good views to the right here towards the army ranges on Tunnel Hill). Keep forward across the next field, later with holly trees on the left, to reach a stile in iron railings and with a stone wall on the left. Cross the stile and keep ahead along the crest of the ridge with a wooden fence on your left. You are on Hazelacre Hill. The path later descends, curving left, still beside the wooden fence to reach a complicated junction of tracks.

Care should be taken here to ensure you go the correct way! Follow the fence left past an Edward VII pillar box on the left above the WD 1290 stone by the entrance to Pirbright Lodge. Ignore a bridleway sign and two footpath signs now on your right, but in another 10 yards turn rightwards up a rough track (no signpost) with a field on your left and common land to the right. At the top of the hill pass 'Admirals Walk', a fine Elizabethan-style house, on the left. Descend through a cutting and continue with a barbed wire fence on the left. Where fence bears left — WD 1295 — bear left with it on to a pleasant track going gently downhill. After 100 yards pass two gates on the left and continue a further 100 yards to a large 'Byelaws' notice on the right. The path then in quick succession turns left behind a holly tree and then rightwards again resuming the original direction, now between rhododendrons (this section can be very muddy after prolonged rain), later with a ditch between barbed wire fences on the left, to reach a single plank bridge across a stream. Cross this and the stile on the other side, and bear very slightly left across the field to another stile on the opposite side. Cross this to enter woodland, and continue ahead on a clear footpath with a ditch on the left to cross yet another small stream by a little hump-backed bridge. Keep forward past a single gatepost on the left and through a strip of young pine trees to emerge on a wide, clear crossing track on Stanford Common.

This is point A and those wishing to shorten the walk should turn left here and follow this track past Stream Farm Kennels on the left to reach the main A324 road opposite the Royal Oak. Turn left along the road — beware of fast traffic — to reach a road junction. Here turn rightwards for Woking and shortly round a left bend to some houses (B). Here rejoin the main walk.

To continue the main walk from point A bear rightwards, later passing a cottage on the right. Keep forward along its drive, which acquires a tarmac surface after a few yards, later with a pond on your right, to reach a lane. Here turn right, and in 250 yards you will reach a gate across the lane at the boundary of the Army's Ash Ranges.

Turn left before the gate on a very wide track and cross a concrete bridge over a stream to a 'Private Lake' sign on a tree. Bear left to another 'Private Lake' sign at a gap in a fence. (Despite all the deterrent signs around here: 'No fishing', 'No bathing' etc, this *is* a public footpath and there is a discreet little sign, which you may not notice as it is placed well up a tree, asking you to keep to the path). Pass through the gap and follow a path through rhododendrons with occasional glimpses of Henleypark Lake to the right. At the corner of the lake cross a concrete bridge over the exit stream and *bear left* to reach a crossing track in 10 yards. Turn rightwards along this. The track soon curves left to another junction where bear rightwards along a track between pine trees and with wooden fence posts on the left. At the first crossing track, turn left, slightly uphill, and keep forward eventually to go through a field gate on to the main A324 road, opposite the main entrance to a factory, seemingly incongruously sited in this rural spot.

Cross the road and turn left on the tarmac pavement which soon curves rightwards away from the road into the factory car park (footpath sign to Cobbett Hill). Keep ahead, making for the far diagonal corner of the car park, ie the left end of the furthermost line of low white rails which mark out the lines of parking places. Here bear rightwards along a clear track along the edge of a wood to reach a clear crossing track (there should be some metal mesh fire beaters standing on the left-hand corner). Turn left here, with the factory behind you, and follow a clear track for nearly ½ mile through Henley Park, noting the views of the Hogs Back and Guildford cathedral to the right, to reach a lane at a white swing-gate. Cross the lane, and follow another clear track opposite for a couple of hundred yards, and then bear left, leaving the main track, on to another track which curves slightly left at first and then runs almost dead straight for ½ mile over Cobbetthill Common. (After ¼ mile you will pass two radio masts on your right.) You will eventually reach the corner of a wire mesh fence on the right (also WD 1372).

Still keep forward, over a stream, and then bear right (WD 1371) to reach a cul-de-sac road with houses on the right. Go forward along this to the main road, where you turn right.

This is point B where those taking the shorter walk rejoin the main route. Keep along the main (B380) road, passing the Research Institute on the right, to a bus stop and wooden shelter on the left at a road junction. Here turn half left, taking the little path on the immediate right of the 'Bullswater Common Road' sign (ignore the bridleway sign pointing up the road) and keep parallel with the road on your left about 20 yards away. Opposite no 11 Bullswater Common Road, the little track you are on veers away to the right, and you should bear left on to the right-hand edge of the wide grass verge of the road, later passing a wooden footpath sign on your right. The road then makes a little S-bend to join the line on which you are already walking. Keep forward to the end of the road and bear slightly right between posts to reach a main road in 50 yards. The word SLOW is painted in the road here.

Turn left for a few yards, and then rightwards down a little lane at a wooden footpath sign on a metal post. After 250 yards pass a bungalow named 'Shebbear' on the left, and in another 20 yards go straight ahead on to a grassy track. In just under 200 yards cross a raised wooden bridge with a stile at either end, and continue over boggy ground for 20 yards (try to walk on the branches and other improvised stepping stones which have been placed in it) and then curve left and proceed slightly uphill towards a large red-brick house seen ahead. On reaching the corner of the garden of this house, keep forward between fences with the garden on your right and a field on the left. Pass the entrance to Hogleys Farm on the left and keep forward beside the hedge to reach a cross track. Here turn left for a few yards, then right at the entrance to Hogleys House on to a tarmac lane. In 100 yards turn left (footpath sign) along an unmade track between cottages and then fields. Pass a house 'Nuthurst' on your right.

In 50 yards turn rightwards along a grassy strip between the hedge on your right (follow this closely) and a flowerbed of the garden of Whites Farm on your left. In 20 yards you come to some rustic fencing. Do *not* climb this, but use the stile now seen on your right to enter a field where there is a footpath sign. Immediately turn left, keeping slightly out from the edge of the field to reach an unusual triangular stile on the far side. Cross it, and a footbridge over a small stream. Bear rightwards, following the direction of another footpath sign, along a narrow path between young trees to reach a third footpath sign apparently pointing left down a grassy ride.

Take great care here; you are nearly at the end of the walk and it would be a pity to go astray now. The sign is not pointing directly down the ride, but at a point about 10 yards down the right-hand side of it. Here you will find a very narrow path bearing right through the trees in exactly the direction of the footpath sign — hopefully pointing the correct way. One can never be sure that a sign has not been twisted round. This little path gradually curves further right and emerges on to a grassy track through a tree nursery. (Please do not touch the plants — they are private property.) Continue past glasshouses on the left to reach a path junction where there is a wooden footpath signpost pointing in the direction from which you have come. Turn left here, and keep right of buildings to join the main drive. Pass a battery chicken shed on the left and you will soon emerge beside the Cricketers on to Pirbright village green, thus completing the walk.

Walk 8   Sunningdale and Chobham Common

8½ miles (13.5 km)

OS sheet 175

This walk can be easily shortened to 4½ miles (7 km).

Chobham Common, resplendent, in season, with gorse and heather, has often been compared with Dartmoor. It is certainly wild country and not one I'd care for you to be on in bad weather or when the shades of night are falling fast. But in fair weather and with good visibility I feel sure you will enjoy it. I have taken particular care, after paying several visits, to describe what should be a trouble-free route.

Sunningdale is on the A30 (T). Park at or close by the railway station.

From the car parks at Sunningdale station proceed to the level crossing and take a path by the side of the signal box. This, rising, crosses a transverse road and brings you to the forward Ridgemount road. Keep along this pleasant residential way and at its end, in about ½ mile, continue (you will be on a public bridleway) by the drive of Sunninghill Golf Club — at first concreted but soon becoming gravelled.

At the first fork bear left, ignoring the half-right branch, soon passing cottages on the right. Then, over footplanks, the heath begins. Keep straight on the sandy track, over any cross paths and rising a little. Through wilder heath the track descends and subsequently makes a left bend.

A few yards after this look out for, and take, a track on the right. It is quite clear but as it is covered by pine needles and a little sombre in consequence, it is quite possible that the eye may be diverted by the forward bright sandy track. So be careful!

This track rises but soon descends slowly and in due course brings you out to a little lane. Wait until you reach it. Do not divert rightwards. Turn left in this lane but in only a few yards turn rightwards on a clear 'ride' through the trees, quite soon to reach a road in which turn rightwards, immediately passing the Brickmakers Arms.

In rather more than a ¼ mile, having passed the clock turret of Ribsden Holt on your right, turn in left, immediately past a cottage, on a signposted public bridleway. Follow this shaded, pretty way round several bends, the last one taking you alongside the M3

31

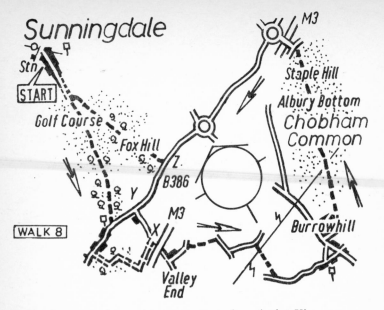

Sunningdale

WALK 8

embankment and so out to a transverse lane (point X).

For the shorter walk turn *left* and on reaching (point Y) a transverse road, at the Convent, turn rightwards. In less than ½ mile you will come, on the right, to a letter box and a sign 'Brick Hill'. This is point Z to which reference will subsequently be made, and where you rejoin the main route.

For the full walk turn rightwards under the motorway arch. Soon take the first left-hand turning, passing the school and then the almost tree-hidden, modern church. Shortly after this, at Pembroke House, slant half rightwards, passing, with wooden rails on your right, Little Pembroke and along a hedged path.

This runs out to a house and is continued forward by a gravelled drive to a transverse lane. Here turn rightwards and at the fork bear to the left, uphill. As you rise note the rearward view of the pretty thatched and half-timbered cottage.

At the top of the rise you will see a public footpath sign on the right. Turn in here (electricity transformer at the corner). Follow the enclosed path, soon under the power line (of which more anon) and via an intermediate iron swing gate, out to a road. Here turn left and, a little later, ignore a right-hand offshoot, and also some footpath offshoots.

The official sign indicates that you are now at Chobham although you are actually at its northern extension — Burrowhill. On reaching the village stores and post office (usual ice cream and soft drinks, if required, but not, apparently, after mid-day Saturday) fork back left to the Four Horseshoes.

Take the little road immediately opposite the inn and on very soon reaching the transverse main road, cross over and take the 'Horse Ride' (so marked). Follow the clear and obvious path, half left over the green to a track or rough road. Here, ignoring the continuation opposite, turn rightwards. Go over a cross track (or rough road) to the red-brick buildings seen ahead. You will find that they are named Killy Hill Cottages. At a lamp-post at the corner turn left and at once take the right-hand fork amd keep to it ignoring a very minor right-hand offshoot. There will soon be a ditch and property boundary fence on your right.

Where your path bears rightwards, bear with it but in only a few yards, near the angle of the right-hand fence, veer half left and so out on to the open common land.

Now take stock of your position so that you can enjoy your traverse of this part of the wild and, in season, beautiful Chobham Common and not be frustrated. In fact, in adverse weather, it is *most important* to appreciate your position.

Ahead you will see the power line. Note, first of all, that if this is followed leftwards (or if you strike off leftwards — westwards — from the route I give) you will arrive safely at a road. (See my map.) So if you do (but why?) get into difficulties, here is your safety line.

But, for the ramble route, note directly ahead, a pylon which I will call 'objective no. 1'. Behind it, a mile ahead, appears a Knoll at Staple Hill recognised by its curious scars.

Though the route may seem complicated, since paths and tracks run hither and yon in an apparently inconsequential way, it should be quite easy if you give every word of the following description its full weight:

Go forward to the corner of a group of conifers.

Pass these on your left.

Cross a broad track.

Go forward for a few yards to meet another cross track.

Turn leftwards in this. It brings you just to the right of the pylon which is objective no. 1. In fact it carries you towards the next pylon.

At a fork just before the power line go left. Ignore a minor rightward footpath.

Pass under the power line and continue by a rising path through the heather.

You come to a wide, almost road-like, cross track. Turn left in it.

Soon, at a 'circus', bear off half right *forward*.

On soon reaching a junction turn squarely right towards the Knoll at Staple Hill (seen ahead).

This wide and clear track, later veering a little to the right, brings you, over a cross track, to Staple Hill which you now very easily ascend to enjoy the extensive view.

Your final objective — a busy road roundabout — can now be seen. To reach it I suggest turning your back to the way you have come and continuing forward, over a cross track, then a little leftwards downhill and into a cross track turning rightwards. So, through posts, out to a road. Turn left and soon bear rightwards over the bridge which spans the M3. Then turn left on the Windlesham road (more or less parallel with the M3).

We must keep on the high road for a while, though die-hards may try to walk on the heath to the left. (Only real experts provided with large-scale map, compass, jungle knife, thigh boots and survival kit would attempt a crossing of the common to the right.) But as we walk along the road we can appreciate the wildness of this part of Chobham Common in a more leisurely way than is possible when driving a car.

In a little under ¾ mile we come to, and continue over, crossroads. In about ½ mile farther you will come to a nameplate 'Brick Hill' and a letter box on the left.

This (point Z) is where those taking the shorter walk rejoin the main route.

A few yards past this spot turn rightwards (don't miss it!) on a woodland path. (If you have taken the shorter walk you will proceed —for locating purposes—to the 'Brick Hill' sign and then turn backwards a few yards.)

This way, though having footpath status only, is an ancient trackway known as the 'Six Foot Way'. Before long it lives up to its name width-wise as it goes through heathland, here rather attractive, and then crosses (white posts give direction) a fairway of the Sunninghill Golf Course. The sandy track goes through another short woodland stretch and again crosses a fairway. Again there is a short woodland stretch and another—this time wider—fairway is crossed. After going yet again through a woodland patch, the track, now grassy, bends a little left.

Whilst one is grateful that there are no minatory notices on the golf course, it might help to prevent inadvertent trespass if there were some discreet signposting or waymarking at this point.

Clearly, however, it is more convenient to all concerned to keep left along the edge of the fairway and with a strip of trees on your left. A little later a fragmented bit of track is seen to the right. By this (and keeping forward again) you reach the main drive along which you came on the outward journey and so retrace a little of your outward way back to the starting point.

Walk 9

Shere and Abinger Hammer

6 miles (9.5 km)

OS sheet 187

With so many other beautiful villages in the county, it would be a confident person who affirmed that Shere was the prettiest of them all. But there is certainly much on which to base the claim. Shere has a lovely situation, being in the valley of the Tilling Bourne, under the steep, well wooded downland escarpment over which we walk on this ramble. It has some lovely old cottages and, suitably facing an ancient oak, the attractive White Horse dating from *c.* 1600 but since refronted and also renovated inside.

Shere is just off the A25, halfway between Dorking and Guildford. The A25 bypasses the village so slant off just after leaving Gomshall.

I found that the best place for parking seemed to be in the recreation ground across the old main road at the northern end of the High Street. There is limited parking space in the village centre but this quickly gets taken up by visitors' cars in the main holiday season. The recreation ground parking is not at all obvious to the casual visitor.

At Shere, go down the High Street and over the Tilling Bourne. Opposite the White Horse turn left, past the war memorial. At the church turn rightwards. Where this little lane soon bends squarely rightwards, turn left on a signposted track.

This is at first hedged both sides. It then becomes open on the right. Later it becomes enclosed again. It is followed unerringly to a transverse little lane on the outskirts of Gomshall.

Turn left and follow round a rightward curve. Go over a cross road. Where the road you are now on makes a square left turn, go rightwards, under the railway arch. Through this, disregard, at once, the first private drive but a few yards farther on turn leftwards on a track, with a farmyard on your right.

Note soon an enclosed footpath on the left running, at first, alongside the farm road. Follow this out to a stony drive. Here keep forward. Where this soon turns squarely right, turn in leftwards, passing a house on your immediate right. Take care, after this, to slant off half right. In practice you will go through a fieldgate (or its opening) though you will see that alongside it is an old wooden swing gate.

Continue by the left-hand side of a field to join a track which takes

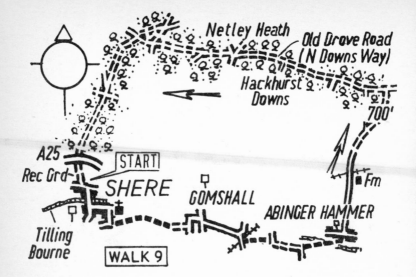

you over the Tilling Bourne and so to the Guildford road. Here turn rightwards, very soon to reach the Abinger Arms at Abinger Hammer about 2½ miles from the start.

From the side of the inn take the traffic-restricted (Hackhurst) lane which (ignore any paths branching off it) rises and then descends to Hackhurst Farm. Beyond this cross (carefully!) the railway.

On my high summer visit I found the hedged trackway ahead initially somewhat grassy but perfectly passable. Before very long it becomes almost a grass-free leafy tunnel — quite clear.

So you plod steadily upwards keeping always to the main track. There will come a time, however, where the forward track has an obviously 'abandoned' look. At this point, but not until then, slant through an opening on the right and at once resume your forward way now, as a reward for your climbing, with a glorious open view on the right. Still rising, continue, sometimes through and sometimes alongside scrub, until you come to an unmistakable transverse track. Here turn left.

Follow this, through scrub mostly, until you come to a clearing. The track, as used by horseriders, goes half left. But you *keep ahead*. There will be a wall-like patch of furze over to your right. You join a better-marked track and pass, on your right, a log seat.

Immediately beyond this, at crossways, turn rightwards on a clear track. At the next crossways turn left and on meeting a transverse track turn rightwards. A track later comes in from the right, but you keep straight on uphill to reach, at a rough road, a 'Surrey County Council: Hackhurst Downs' sign.

Here turn left and follow the forestry road slightly downhill soon passing on the left the National Trust's sign 'Little Kings Wood'. From here is a good view with Hindhead clearly seen to the south-south-west.

Resuming our way we come to, and ignore, a pair of right-hand offshoots. Now rising gently we presently come to an earth track which strikes off on the right. Take this, a pine wood on the right and bracken on the left, out to a rough road in which bear rightwards. A lane comes in from the right and a Y-junction follows. Here, with a static water tank opposite, is a four-way signpost. Take the public bridleway, so indicated, for Shere, ie left at the fork.

You go, by a line of water tanks, through the lofty pines. On meeting a transverse way, cross over (a National Trust sign indicates 'Netley Park') and take the forward way through the woods, now definitely descending. Avoid a half-left fork. Keep straight on, past a war-time blockhouse where disregard a leftward turn. Tantalizing peeps of open country appear on the left and you will probably note, later, a small gap from which there is a most delightful view of Shere in the valley.

Thus you continue by the 'hollow' way (held together, seemingly, by the fantastically gnarled roots of the great trees), under the road bridge and so out to the Shere Recreation Ground and back to Shere village again.

Note Gomshall is usually pronounced *Gumms'll* and Abinger is pronounced *Abbinjer*.

Walk 10   Shere and the Silent Pool

3½ miles (5.5 km)

OS sheet 187

Apart from the delights of Shere and the Tilling Bourne (see notes
to Walk 9) there is the added interest on this walk of the Silent
Pool, one of the two ponds attached to Sherbourne Farm. Whoever
cooked up the name did a very good public relations job. But he who
put out the trite legend — that a peasant girl, to escape the lecherous
attentions of King John who happened to be passing by, preferred
drowning (an unlikely happening in such a shallow pool) to
dishonour, would have been told by my English master at school:
'Can do better'.

Yet, even when there is an influx of visitors, the pool, mirroring
the trees which thickly surround it, is strangely beautiful. I strongly
advise you to approach by the walk route here described. But you
could base the walk on the Silent Pool — there is a car park nearby.
You could then find out whether the farm tea-house is open and
whether you could count on refreshment when you return.

For directions to Shere, see Walk 9.

For the Silent Pool direct, continue on the A25. The Sherbourne
Farm drive (entrance to the Silent Pool) and car park, lie
immediately past the Albury (A248) road.

Assuming you are starting from the Shere Recreation Ground (make
adjustments if you are parking elsewhere) turn rightwards in the road
on leaving. Follow round a right-hand bend. At 'Upper Lodge'
take a 'made' path between white metal posts and follow out to the
Guildford (A25) road. Cross to, and go up the road opposite. In
about ⅜ mile, after a left-right bend and where the road starts to
run through a wood, you will find on the left a 'Surrey County
Council Open Space' sign and also a 'Public Bridleway' post.

Fork off here. The way (by a wood's edge) goes uphill by a
reasonably easy gradient, with delightful views to reward your
efforts.

At the top there is an unmistakable transverse track. Turn leftwards along this, with plantation on the right and narrow belt of
trees on the left. Before long you will come to a definite cross track.
Here turn leftwards, downhill. This is a most delightful 'hollow'
way with fine trees. But the oft-repeated statement that the way has
been worn concave by the passage of countless visitors to the Silent

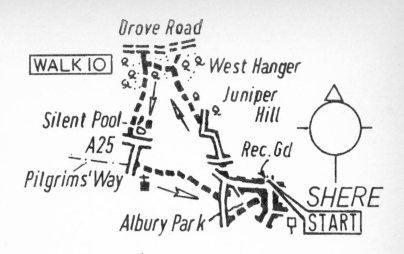

Pool is surely an example of guidebook writers cribbing each other's work without a personal check and evaluation on the site. For this is a comparatively unknown 'back' way. One imagines visitors of a former generation came in horse-drawn conveyances along the Guildford road, even as present-day visitors come by car.

The woodland track gives on to an enclosed path, open country to the right. At its end there is a sudden left turn. Immediately round this, on the left, is an iron swing gate which gives entry to the Silent Pool.

Having looked round (one can circle the lake) proceed to the farm, ie turn left on quitting the Silent Pool enclosure and bear rightwards out to the A25, here a dual carriageway. Cross over and turn left. Soon turn rightwards for Albury. By the bus stop one can take a path which runs by the side of the road. Soon, at a VR letterbox, turn left. The hedged track soon brings you to a stile by a gate. Cross the meadow to a point just rightwards of the far left-hand corner.

Follow the path through the re-afforested Silver Wood, ignoring a left-hand fork, to leave by an iron swing gate. Keep forward still, over a meadow and, at a copse, reach an iron swing gate and emerge on a minor road.

Here turn rightwards, soon past a black-and-white framed house.

After crossing the Tilling Bourne turn left (river on left). Keep always forward, soon by an avenue and then by a road, back into Shere centre again.

Walk 11

6 miles (9.5 km)

Shere and Newlands Corner

OS sheet 187

Newlands Corner, 567 ft up on a crisply-turfed crest of the North Downs, is well known to motorists as a place of wide views with parking and picnicking facilities. As beautiful as the view is, however, we may not be loath to leave it for quieter ways. Notes on Shere and Albury appear with other walks in this book.

The start is at Shere, directions to which can be found in Walk 9. It may be remarked, however, that as this is a circular walk it could be started also from the car parks at Newlands Corner or at West Hanger. The latter is comparatively unknown.

Enter the recreation ground at Shere but almost at once leave it to take a hedged bridleway running to its left and just outside it. It is decidedly 'hollow' way. You subsequently pass under the bridge which carries the A25. Just after this turn sharply left and, in a few yards, turn rightwards (resuming your former way) with wire and an open field on your left.

The way steadily rises. At a war-time blockhouse the way divides. Keep ahead, ie take the left fork, with the wire fence still on your left. The way is temporarily narrower.

You enter woodland and pass, on your right, a small wired-off reservoir. An open field again appears on the left and you continue by the left-hand wire. The bridleway then makes a slight half-right bend and once more continues by the left-hand wire. The buildings of Hollister Farm are seen ahead.

Go over a cross-track and continue in the farm drive opposite. Disregard branches to the left. Continue out to a road in which turn rightwards for a couple of dozen yards or so. Then turn back sharply left on a woodland bridleway. You soon come to and cross a road.

Here is the *West Hanger* car park, an *alternative start* to the walk. Go straight through the car park and continue by the woodland way. It is an ancient drove road. In ⅜ mile or so, you come to a ground-level 'Public Bridleway' signstone. Disregard the left-hand offshoot here. Keep straight on. At the next definite fork disregard the slightly downhill left-hand branch. Take the *forward* course, very slightly rightwards of your previous direction but avoiding a definite right-hand branch. Keep forward all the way to the main road (A25) at Newlands Corner, another *alternative start*.

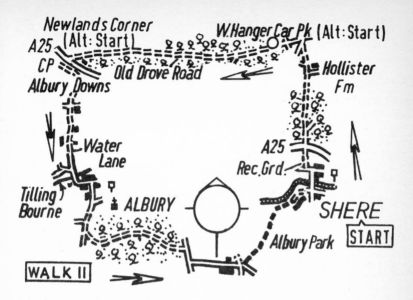

Turn rightwards and opposite the 'Barn' cafe turn leftwards in the car park and picnic area approach. In only a few yards turn leftwards through the posts and take a stony track. It is along here that you can enjoy the wonderful view away from the crowds. The general direction to take lies along the obvious track. But note that just to the left of this, and parallel to it there is a path at a higher level which gives superior views. The main track is in a hollow.

You subsequently join the main track and at a Y-fork turn rightwards. One will appreciate the ensuing romantic sunken way if one is well shod. This stony way is no place for thin peep-toe sandals.

You subsequently cross a transverse way, disregarding a left-hand branch; the Pilgrims' Way incidentally. Your way is forward, at first with a wooded bank on the right.

Your way is no longer so rough but lane-like. Farms and cottages are then passed and so you come to a T-junction and learn that you have been going along Water Lane — a no-through-road for motorists. You are now on the outskirts of Albury.

Turn left, soon over the Tilling Bourne. The Drummond Arms lies ahead but, for the walk, turn rightwards (for the church) at the old signpost opposite the post office. Disregard the next left turn. Keep straight on in Blackheath Lane, 'Impassable For Motorists'. The way goes through quite a deep sandstone cutting as it rises.

After passing a large concrete dutch barn on the right look out for and take a very sandy left-hand fork. A nice view (albeit with pig pens in the foreground) opens up on the right. The track then enters

41

woodland and you follow out, disregarding a pair of stiles at the side. The way then becomes quite wide and, by a metal gate, you reach a clearing. Here keep by the left-hand edge and, now joining a rough little lane, follow out to a road.

Here turn rightwards and very soon turn left in Park Road. Disregard a minor right-hand offshoot. Just after passing cottages on the right, you come to a road angle. Here, immediately *past* the house on the left, take the signposted *footpath* from a swing gate and so enter Albury Park. The path goes forward between a line of limes on your left and some on your right, though these latter soon cease.

Ahead you will see a wired-off sheep compound. Pass this on your immediate right. You come to a good stile and continue to a lodge which has been seen conspicuously ahead. Pass this on your immediate right and so come out on a bridleway with the Tilling Bourne ford immediately ahead—a pretty spot and a cool one in warm weather.

Without crossing the stream, turn rightwards with the water on your immediate left. A little later bear half left on an avenue and, over a cross way, continue soon with the Tilling Bourne again on your immediate left, into Shere centre again.

Walk 12   Gomshall and The Hackhurst Downs

4 miles (6.5 km)

OS sheet 187

When I was exploring the Shere district I found several ways of getting on to the hills from the valley below. This walk is planned to include a way up and a way down not covered in other rambles. Those who have done the other walks will not mind, I am sure, doing the short section along the old drove road and the equally short section along the Tilling Bourne valley again, especially as these are given in the reverse direction, offering different views.

Gomshall lies on the A25 between Dorking and Guildford. Park discreetly in village, especially in lanes off the main road.

From Gomshall take the footpath leading off the A25 just to the left of the Downside Service Station a few yards from the junction with Queen Street. The path takes you up a few steps and then goes up the side of a valley.

In ⅜ mile and at a fork, a little after passing a house on the right, bear squarely rightwards and continue upwards through the trees until meeting a clear crossing track. Here turn rightwards among trees, disregarding a backward-slanting downhill path on the right.

The track narrows to a path and continues gently downhill, passing a grey house to the left. You come out on a small lane, signposted to Colekitchen Farm, in which turn left.

After passing the farm on your left continue uphill until reaching a junction of tracks at the top known as Gravehill Gate. Here turn rightwards and follow the broad track, which is an old drove road, now forming part of the North Downs Way, for about ¾ mile until the track seems to divide. Here go rightwards for a few yards and pass between some posts. Then take rightwards the path just to the right of the Surrey CC's 'Hackhurst Downs' sign. Proceed downhill, keeping rightwards at a fork. The path winds about as it descends and offers some fine views over the valley below.

Keep following the path down the hillside until joining a track in which continue to go downhill. Just after passing under a railway arch a farm track comes in from the left. Continue forward, however, out to the main road (the A25). Here turn leftwards and, in 200 yards, opposite Hatch Farm, turn rightwards on a track and almost at once fork rightwards again towards some houses. Keep on past these and over the Tilling Bourne.

ABINGER HAMMER

Just before the track rises and the surface becomes partly concreted go half left to a small gate. Through this, follow the path slightly uphill, soon along the right-hand side of a field. You thus arrive at a gate by a house. Continue on the track ahead. It soon meets another and in this you bear rightwards.

Just after passing a bungalow on the left the stony track bends to the right. At this point take the tarmac enclosed path ahead. Follow this out, through a couple of swing gates and then alongside a farm road, out to a road.

Here turn rightwards to pass under the railway arch. Immediately beyond this turn left. At the next T-junction turn rightwards and so back to your starting point at Gomshall.

Walk 13

5 miles (8 km)

OS sheet 186

Godalming and Eashing

The two Eashing bridges met on this walk, with their small round arches, crossing separate channels of the Wey, are of thirteenth-century foundation and, with the adjacent row of sixteenth-century half-timbered cottages, are in custody of the National Trust, which has put up an explanatory plaque.

Our route takes us as near as we are allowed to the 1765 mansion of Peper Harow. Although it is pronounced 'Pepper Harrow' note the spelling.

If you have time to spare at the end of the walk, a stroll around Godalming can be quite pleasant. Even an ad-lib exploration will reveal much of interest and beauty though a guide book will give details. Do not overlook a short walk along the Wey and Arun canal (see notes to Walk 4).

Godalming is on the A3100 via Guildford. For this walk we use the Crown Court car park just off the High Street.

From the Crown Court car park just off the High Street, turn left into the Burys. Where the road turns to the left take the path on the right through the churchyard. At the fork, just before the church is reached, keep right and follow out to a road in which turn rightwards. Follow over the River Wey and under a railway bridge to a tarmac path on the left signposted to Hurtmore and Shackleford. This soon crosses a factory road and continues ahead with, after a while, the River Wey on your left. Follow the path out to a road.

Turn left and where the road ends continue straight ahead along a signposted track. For a while this is fairly narrow but broadens again after passing a house on the left. It subsequently becomes a tarmac lane and is followed out to a road (Hurtmore Road) with the Squirrel almost opposite.

Turn left here and at the main road cross to Elstead Road opposite. Follow the path running rightwards of and parallel to the road to a junction by a pillar box. Here turn rightwards on the track signed for 'Moorcroft'. After passing the second house on the left continue ahead along an enclosed path. At the end of the wood on your left and at a T-junction turn left and with the wood on your left and open countryside to your right follow the track out to a road.

Turn rightwards in the road and go along this to the junction in

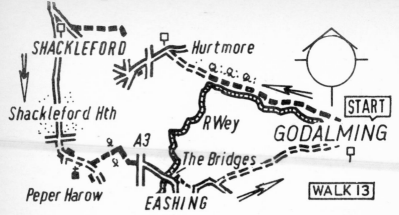

Shackleford by a telephone box. Turn sharp left here into Peper Harow passing the 'Cyder House' on the left. Continue up the road for about ¾ mile until reaching a crossing road. Here go over to the swing gate just to the left of a signpost. Go through this and continue ahead to a tarmac drive. Follow this down through the estate village of Peper Harow noting, on the left, the mellowed seventeenth-century granary raised on stilts hopefully to protect it from the depredations of rodents.

Just after passing St Nicholas Church (with some interesting brasses though the church is usually locked) on the right, you come to a gateway. Take the swing gate, with a 'Public Footpath' sign, to the left of this and follow the direction of the sign over the field.

On meeting the corner of a field (on your left) continue with the wire fence (left) to a stile by a line of trees. Cross this and also a second stile a few yards farther. Now turn right for a few yards, go through a swing gate and turn left to follow the wire fence on your left. Follow this around a square right bend, passing through a gate and on down to a fork. Go left past a one-bar swing gate and follow the path out to a road (A3).

Cross this and take the road almost opposite into Eashing. After crossing the second bridge turn left on to a path which soon starts to climb the bank to the right. At the top cross a stile and follow the path with a wire fence on your left out to a road. Turn left along this and follow round a sharp right bend and continue until reaching Halfway Lane on your left. Turn left along this and continue straight ahead to a road corner. Keep straight ahead again, passing a house on your left, out to a road and continue downhill.

Follow this road under a railway bridge and shortly after it joins another bear left along Station Approach. At the T-junction cross to the churchyard opposite and from here it is a short way back to the car park.

46

Walk 14   Hurtwood Common and
                                              Holmbury Hill

5½ miles (9 km)

OS sheet 187

Gibbet Hill, Hindhead (see Walk 2) is, at 895 ft, the second highest hill in Surrey, the pride of place being taken by Leith Hill at 965 ft (see Walk 19). But the second and third highest summits in the Leith Hill range are, respectively, Holmbury Hill at 857 ft and Pitch (Coneyhurst) Hill at 844 ft. On this present walk we go over the tops of Leith Hill's two lofty neighbours. As may be expected, wonderful views, hardly less sweeping than those enjoyed from Leith Hill itself, are to be obtained. We go through extensive woodland areas, old and new. If you follow my directions carefully you will not get lost. But an OS map and a pocket compass are useful to have on woodland walks well off the roads, where in the interests of forestry management, new tracks, firebreaks, clearing and the like may be made.

Our first objective is Peaslake village. This lies in quite a tangle of lanes so that some careful map reading and attention to signposts is called for. One way would be to branch southwards off the A25 (Dorking-Guildford road) at Gomshall. Soon you go over the railway level crossing. On reaching the war memorial at Peaslake village be sure to pass the Hurtwood Inn on your *immediate right*. Continue for about 1½ miles to the easily-identified Windmill inn and then turn backwards for about 300 yards. A car parking space (unheralded by any sign or notice) will now be on your right.

Having parked the car, continue through the car park to a bridle-way. Where this forks, bear left.

In about ¾ mile, just past a right-hand forestry road and as the bridleway emerges into a bracken-covered clearing, a path crosses at right angles. Here turn rightwards uphill, shortly crossing a forestry road.

At the top of the hill the path merges with a broader track. Go forward, soon dropping steeply downhill (take care after wet weather!) to a farm track in which turn left.

Follow out to a road in which turn leftwards. In about 150 yards (by a holly bush) take a narrow path on the right. This goes uphill and crosses a road. Keep straight on, ignoring all side paths until you come to an 'island' of three young trees where you turn right.

Again keep forward. In about ⅓ mile a track crosses at right

47

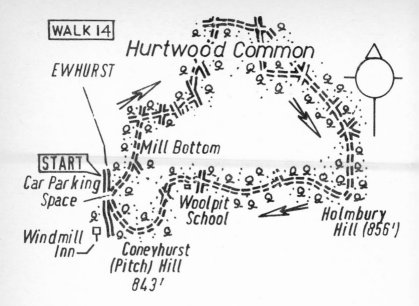

WALK 14

Hurtwood Common

EWHURST

Mill Bottom

START
Car Parking
Space

Windmill
Inn

Coneyhurst
(Pitch) Hill
843'

Woolpit
School

Holmbury
Hill (856')

angles. At this point, as a check on your position, you will see, on the left, a couple of water board red and white posts.

Turn, however, *rightwards*. You'll pass more of these bi-coloured posts from time to time.

At a crossing path by a fire hydrant cover turn left. Disregard all crossing paths until, after about ¾ mile, you will find a fire warning notice (Hurtwood Control) on a tree. Here also are overhead power lines.

Here bear a trifle rightwards on a fine broad track with the power lines to your left. Where the path narrows bear rightwards. The view begins to open up on your left and the path gradually ascends to the summit of Holmbury Hill.

Here we find a circular memorial seat. Leaving this on our left we cross the open space and come to two paths. We take the leftmost, slightly downwards around the edge of the hill, ignoring all paths to the right and left.

The path then veers rightwards. At a T-junction we turn left on the prominent main path but immediately take a wide rightward, downhill, fork.

On coming to a row of concrete blocks, turn left to pass an open space on the right. Continue to a narrow tarmac road. Here turn rightwards and, in only a few yards, turn leftwards, slightly downhill through the trees.

Where the path bears left, turn rightwards through a gate and thence to a stile which gives on to an enclosed path which crosses the valley. When you find this path going slightly uphill to hollies, keep straight ahead and so out to a road, opposite the Woolpit School lodge.

Cross and go by the drive leftwards of the lodge. Where this drive bears left we leave it and continue by an uphill path with a sports field to our right. Continue up to a break in the boundary fence.

Our chosen path bears left, uphill, and brings us to a prominent track in which we turn left. At an early fork we bear rightwards through mixed woodland.

At a subsequent cross track turn left to arrive at an open area. On a fine day you can see, if not forever, at least the South Downs just over 20 miles away.

Continuing, keeping to the left in the edge of the hill we come to the open space which is the summit (at the OS triangulation pedestal) of Pitch (or Coneyhurst) Hill (843 ft).

By the sandy track continue ahead to a fork. Here we bend rightwards and, soon, pass an old quarry.

Leaving this on our right we plunge downhill to the car park we started from.

Walk 15   Reynards Hill and Winterfold Forest

4 miles (6.5 km)

OS sheet 187

This is mainly a walk in the Forestry Commission's territory but it is not a case of being unable to see the wood for the trees. The undulating rides, paths and tracks are quite varied, some being exceptionally wide, to act as firebreaks one presumes. In season colour is provided by the bracken and heather, bilberries ('hurts') and the like.

It has to be realized that trees are as much a crop as wheat or potatoes and the only possible one in many cases. Although these walks are intended entirely for recreation, not education, your walks through the newer forests might be made even more enjoyable and interesting if you had a small pocket guide to the many kinds of pines, firs, larches, birches and so on. There is also the animal and bird life of the forest to look out for.

At the start of this walk we go through some older woodland (long may it remain untouched) and have a surprise view. We also pass a little-known windmill, complete with sails.

To make for variety, however, and to carry away an unforgettable impression of some wonderful forest country, I most strongly advise followers of this mainly forest route to complete it by an ascent of Pitch Hill as described in due place.

To arrive at the start follow the directions for Walk 14 (also, refer to the introduction of Walk 14 for advice about direction checking in woodlands).

Leave the car park to cross the lane and take the *leftmost* of the two paths which present themselves. You pass Mill Cottage on your immediate left after which the rising path becomes, for a short time, almost a trench. After going round a fallen tree you come to the top of Windmill Hill. Here is the windmill which gives the hill (and the pub) its name. It is complete with sails and is used, I understand, as a private residence.

Take now the track marked 'To Four Winds Cottages'. Don't take the eye-catching, gravelling, drive-like track. Our chosen track has, initially, a fence on the left. Keep straight on, downhill, out to a lane, disregarding a private left-hand entry.

Turn left and (point X) at once disregard another lane with a 'Road Narrows' sign. Immediately past this you will find a small car

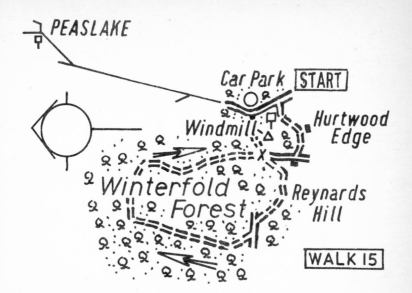

parking space. Enter this and at once bear half-right on a clear, gradually rising, track.

This brings you out to a clearing at the top of Reynards Hill. Through breaks in the trees there is a good view. Bear now rightwards along the wooded edge of the hill, disregarding any minor right-hand paths. Through the trees and especially in winter the view is continued. Hascombe Hill is not far off whilst in the distance one sees the Hindhead range.

So round bends we reach a lane and turn left in it, downhill. Before long, at a slight S-bend, we see two prominent paths striking off on the right. Take the *second* of these, ie go half rightwards of your forward road approach.

Your way is now over Winterfold Heath. A track presently comes in from the left. Here turn rightwards. Ignore, in quick succession, two tracks on the right (they are two heads of the same track). A wide track swings leftwards but do not take it. Cross, instead, to a woodland track opposite, quite clear when you are on it but not immediately obvious.

Subsequently go over a cross path and continue out to a very wide track — a forest firebreak I presume. Turn leftwards in it down to a gate. To the right of this is another gate with a 'Forestry Commission: Winterfold Wood' sign. Next leftward to this is the head of a green track signposted 'Bridle Road to Farley Green'. Take this. Quite soon, however, it loses its old identity and merges with a very wide track along which you proceed.

Now although the subsequent tracks are quite clear and present no difficulty it is most essential that you keep tabs on the various crossings and forks. For this reason I have widely spaced out the following text:

In the broad track keep on, subsequently over a crossing track.

Where a track slants in from the left, turn rightwards, gradually rising.

Subsequently go over a cross track (note view rearwards).

In a few yards continue over another cross track (quite wide).

Where the track ends at a T-junction turn left. You will note, over the clearing, a pleasing view leftwards.

Descend into a dip and then go upward. Keep rightwards at the fork ahead.

Go over a cross path. Descend, fairly steeply and roughly, to a valley track. Turn rightwards.

Keep on, over a minor cross track, out to a lane.

Cross to the lane (point X on the map) with the 'Lane Narrows' sign. Proceed downhill. In a ¼ mile or so, opposite a house named 'Horseblock Hollow' with its conspicuous steps, turn left on a drive-like track. Follow it out (with peeps of open country — into Sussex — on the right) to a lane by the 'Windmill'. Here turn left soon to reach the car park.

To conclude (optionally) with an ascent of Pitch Hill, turn sharply rightwards on entering the car park from the road, initially parallel with the lane you have just quitted but soon curving away from it, uphill, past an old quarry on the left. And so to the OS triangulation pillar at the top of Pitch Hill.

Walk 16   Polesden Lacey and Ranmore Common

6 miles (9.5 km)

OS sheet 187

Polesden Lacey is a delightful Regency (1824) house. In 1923 the Duke (later King George VI) and the Duchess of York spent part of their honeymoon here.

The mansion was bequeathed to the National Trust in 1942 and is much visited for its paintings, furnishing, porcelain and the like.

The magnificent grounds are usually open even when the house itself is not and we are thus enabled to use the car park (but see note at end). The view from the terrace (along which we walk) is superb.

To arrive at Polesden Lacey take the A246 to Great Bookham and here turn southwards and soon, on a drive, westwards. The way is signposted. Park at Polesden Lacey.

From the car park at Polesden Lacey, continue the line of drive by which you approached. Where this soon bends left, leave it to *continue forward* over the grass, passing the house over to your right. You reach a yew hedge and turn left, through a pair of Classical pillars, on to the magnificent terrace walk.

Follow this out, leaving by a Classical arch and now continuing in the drive, which at one point bridges the bridleway below, round bends and out, by a lodge, to a lane. Here turn rightwards. Disregard, very soon (point Y) a right-hand offshoot. Carry on in the valley road for rather over ¼ mile and then turn rightwards.

Immediately you have passed the group of cottages turn left over a stepless bar stile by a field gate. Go by the left-hand hedge. The path/track subsequently veers a little left and brings you, at a wood, to an enclosed path which follows just inside the wood's edge. Towards the end you will have to detour a little rightwards. But rejoin the original line of path and leave by a stile.

In the cow meadow thus reached keep forward more or less parallel to the woodland 'bay' over to your right to arrive at a stile giving on to an enclosed bridleway. Here turn sharp right.

On the preceding section you will have had a first-rate view of Box Hill ahead.

The bridleway you are now on rises steadily. Go over a cross track. It later goes round a leftward bend and you subsequently

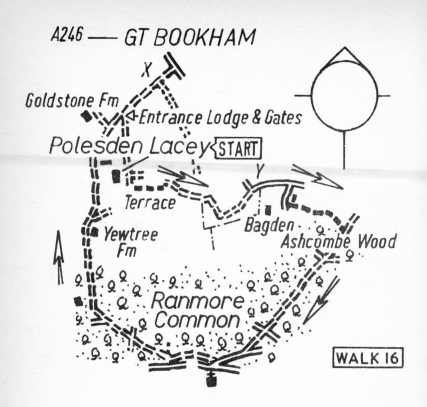

A246 — GT BOOKHAM

Goldstone Fm

Entrance Lodge & Gates

Polesden Lacey START

Terrace

Yewtree Fm

Bagden

Ashcombe Wood

Ranmore Common

WALK 16

come out, the ground having now levelled out, to a small clearing and track junction. Keep forward and take the right-hand of the two forks now presenting themselves, ie you pass an electricity pole with a blue waymark on your immediate *left*.

Follow the clear and delightful track through the bracken. Subsequently go over a crossing road and continue to the next. Here turn rightwards, keeping, of course, on the wide grass verge. Ranmore church is seen ahead by the roadside. It is a landmark for miles around as it is loftily placed and has a graceful tall spire.

Just after passing the church continue by the obvious track which slants a *trifle* rightwards. You rejoin the road and continue past cottages on the right. Immediately past the last of these ignore a track, signposted for Tanners Hatch Youth Hostel and which carries a yellow waymark, going squarely right. Instead, take, adjacently, the *half right* rutted track through the woods. Follow over one cross-track. You descend to, and go over another cross-track. Continue,

54

now rising a little. You will soon pass, on your immediate left, a wire-netted conifer plantation and come out on to a small clearing.

Now be careful! Continue forward soon to reach and join a track which slants in acutely from the left. Keep trees on your left and in only a few yards turn left. Do *not* go along another, more rightward, track headed by a polite sign 'No Horses Please'. In about 85 *steps* (not *strides!*) you come to prominent cross-tracks. Here turn rightwards. The bridleway, for such it technically is, becomes practically a farm road soon with a fine view over to the right and you pass Yewtree Farm on your immediate right.

A little beyond this slant off on a left-hand fork — a clear but narrower, hedged track. As, after descending, it starts to rise, you will find — a pleasant surprise, I hope — that you are now on a kind of causeway lined with yews. You emerge on an angle of drive and continue forward. The sunken way, walled both sides, is spanned by a bridge seen ahead.

Carry on past cottages on the right and continue forward in the bridleway which follows. Just after passing the left-hand bridleway for Goldstone Farm you come to the entrance to Polesden Lacey.

Note The first stage of this walk goes over National Trust property at Polesden Lacey. Should it ever happen that the grounds themselves are closed, proceed as follows. (This is part of a route given in Walk 17 but is repeated here to eliminate possibly confusing cross-reference.)

From the Polesden Lacey gates retrace your way and in ¼ mile, just before coming to the road from Great Bookham, turn rightwards (point X) on a signposted bridleway and follow it out between hedges, veering a little rightwards where a fork offers itself. At one point you pass under an arch which carries the Polesden Lacey drive.

Quite soon after quitting the woodlands, and where the track you are now on bears half rightwards, look out for, and get over a stile on the left. From this point a grassy track brings you to Bagden Farm seen ahead. Turn left in the farm road out (point Y) to a lane. Here turn rightwards and continue with the main ramble.

This is another walk in the delightful Dorking country. We again start from Polesden Lacey but it is to be noted that this time we skirt the estate by a public bridleway. (The drives *inside* the park must be regarded as technically permissive only, though it is unlikely that the National Trust would deny access.)

We pass through a part of Norbury Park (see notes to Walk 23). Although our planned route does not actually go *through* the famous Druids Grove, there is an opportunity of making a slight diversion to see this random hillside avenue of ancient yews, some of grotesque shape and great size.

To arrive at Polesden Lacey follow the directions for Walk 16. Park at Polesden Lacey.

Note that as this is a circular walk it could alternatively be based on Norbury Park.

From the car park at Polesden Lacey retrace your way along the avenue by which you entered. At the top turn rightwards in the road and in ¼ mile (point X) turn rightwards on a signposted bridleway. Follow this out between hedges, veering a little rightwards where a fork seems to offer itself. At one point you pass under an archway which carries the Polesden Lacey drive.

On finally quitting the wood, continue forward for a short distance to a point where the track bends half rightwards. Here look for and get over a stile on the left. From here a grassy track leads (as I found and hope it long remains so) through the cropped field to Bagden Farm seen ahead. Go through the farmyard and in the farm road reached turn left soon to reach a lane in which turn rightwards.

In ¼ mile or so, immediately after passing a right-hand turn, take a path on the left. Be prepared, now, for a stiff climb. But take it easy. Rest frequently to enjoy the ever-expanding fine view rearwards. You could soon imagine yourself to be in a helicopter.

The path, initially a bit lush in high summer but soon clearing, runs with a wire fence on the left and woodland on the right. You subsequently come to a point where the way immediately forward comes to an end but a clear path strikes off rightwards. Turn right *for about 10 yards only.* Then turn left more or less resuming your previous way.

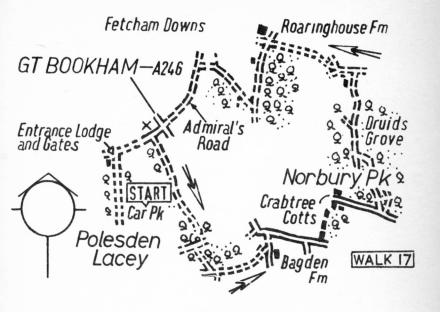

The path (steep!) through the dark trees seems permanently covered with a layer of leaves but 'daylight at the end of the tunnel' is soon seen. Near the top of the rise disregard a 'waymarked' path on the left. The path, now levelling off, then runs, in bends, round a cow pasture, enclosed between a hedge on the right and wire on the left. One hopes that the regular use of this popular path will prevent it from becoming overgrown.

On reaching a flint-walled cottage turn rightwards, passing Crabtree Cottages (what a fine view the owners enjoy!) on the right and a ruined flint building on the left.

You are now on a drive-like little road which runs downhill with exquisite views. In about ⅜ mile from Crabtree Cottages you come, on the left, to an unobstrusive entrance to the Norbury Park estate—signalized, currently, by a framed map and a litter basket. (If you find you are passing the entrance to Foxbury, you have just overshot the mark.)

Turn in here (left) and at once take the left-hand old carriage drive ignoring the right-hand track. At first this 'made' drive runs parallel to the (Crabtree) lane by which you have just approached but soon veers rightwards and later takes a leftward curve. On

57

reaching a transverse drive turn rightwards. Later disregard a half-left fork.

The open woodland on your right is the famous Druids Grove and, if you care to do so, you can detour rightwards to admire the fine old trees. But for the main ramble route, keep straight ahead. The terrain on the right then becomes more open and you pass estate cottages on the left.

At a transverse track turn left. Disregard, very soon, a half-right branch. A tree at its corner has an old red 'waymark'. Keep forward for a few more yards. Then you will come to an open space and keep along its right-hand edge passing a stand of birches to the left and so out to a track. Here turn rightwards.

This is a kind of 'dual bridleway' (hard and soft) which brings you to Roaringhouse Farm. Here turn left on a rough farm road, *not* on the acutely left path into the woods. You pass a farm on the right and here ignore a rightward offshoot. The forward way goes with a wood on the left and a vast open field on the right. At the end of the latter turn very acutely rightwards, now going by another edge of the large field. Keep on, ignoring a path on the left.

After you have passed the power line, there is a very good view despite the fact that much-built-up latter-day Bookham lies immediately ahead. In fact, by a rough stony track we almost reach houses. Just before them, however, we turn left on a fine hedged bridleway called the Admiral's Road. (One would like to imagine a retired old 'Kiss me, Hardy' type pacifically plodding his way along this, his favourite, way.)

On reaching a transverse road cross over and continue by an avenue which runs forward but to the right of and parallel to the Polesden Lacey road. Soon turn left to join this latter road and then go forward, back to the head of Polesden Lacey drive and back to the car park.

Walk 18   Wotton Hatch and Friday Street

3 miles (5 km)

OS sheet 187

In general principle this walk is somewhat similar to no 22 in that it starts from the Guildford (A25) road and again makes for Friday Street. The paths used on what might be called this 'classic' route are quite different, however, and one can never visit delectable Friday Street too many times. For a note on this famed beauty spot see Walk 19.

On this walk we catch the merest glimpse of Wotton House, home of the Evelyns since the sixteenth century but now a Fire Service College. We see all around us, however, the work started by John Evelyn the famous diarist and enthusiastic tree planter; the author of *Sylva: A Discourse on Forest Trees*, among other things, dedicated to King Charles II. Sir John claimed that as a result of this work, millions of trees had been planted in the country. If we may judge by the work of the latter-day Forestry Commission and others in this Abinger State Forest area alone, the idea has taken root in more than one sense of the word.

If you have time and inclination after the walk, a visit to Wotton church is recommended. Apart from its architectural interest and monuments, one appreciates the beauty of its siting—delightfully on a knoll against the backdrop of the Downs. From the hotel, either go a few yards in the Guildford direction and then take a footpath on the right, thereafter going half-right to join a drive, or else go a few yards in the Dorking direction and then take, left, the chestnut avenue to the church.

Wotton Hatch Hotel, where this walk starts, is on the A25 (Guildford) road west of Dorking.

The hotel pub has a good car park and it may be expedient to use this (by arrangement). But as this is a circular walk it can be started at Friday Street (see Walk 19) where there is a large public car park.

From the left-hand side of the Wotton Hatch Hotel as you face it take the *lane*. In about ¼ mile you pass a lodge on the left. Disregard the 'Pheasant Wood' drive here.

The little lane descends in a 6:1 gradient, between sandbanks. Just *past* a cottage ('Damphurst') in the dip, but just *before* a private road on the left, get over a stile on the right. The path (half

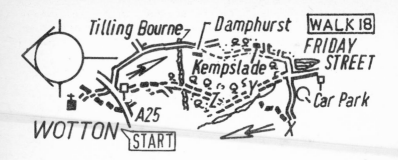

right of the lane direction) is initially grassy but very soon becomes a woodland track running parallel to, but above, the lane below.

A little later the track bears half right away from the lane. Keep forward, ie ignore a right-hand offshoot. The track then becomes a typical Forestry Commission one. At a T-junction turn left. A little later disregard, in quick succession, a left-hand and a right-hand offshoot.

Continue forward with an open field over to your left, out, by a stile by a fieldgate, at Kempslade Farm. Here turn rightwards on the drive which soon meets an elbow of lane. By keeping forward you soon reach the delectable Friday Street pond.

For the ramble route, after the road from Kempslade Farm has bent rightwards, you soon turn rightwards in a little byway bearing a sign 'Wotton Estate: Private Road' but there is a permissive pedestrian way. There will be a wall letter box at the corner.

I might add, however, that there is an alternative way. For this, instead of going down the estate road, continue straight on in the public road, disregarding the left-hand lakeside branch. You pass the car park on your left and in ¼ mile or so past this take (point X) a path on the right which slants back very acutely from the road. Don't go up the farm drive. The path through the woods brings you to a cross-track (point Y) in which turn left.

If we have taken the estate road, however, we find a babbling brook crossing our path and come, in ¼ mile, to point Y where a track comes in from the left. Keep straight on in the beautiful track. In a further ¼ mile look out for point Z, a half-right path (see note at end). Follow it up and then down, over a cross-path through woodland. You may note some yellow waymarks.

On leaving the woods, the path runs ahead between wire, over the Tilling Bourne, and on again through more woodland to reach, at a stile, an open meadow. The Wotton Hatch Hotel is seen half-right ahead and you reach it via its car park.

60

Note If you *should* miss the junction at point Z (though this isn't likely) and find youself on a 'made' drive, do not worry. Just follow its bends (you will be on a public right of way). Note, however, that just after leaving woodland you must take a stile on the right, and so to the hotel. The right of way in the drive does *not* extend out to the road.

Walk 19   Friday Street and Leith Hill

6 miles (9.5 km)

OS sheet 187

I am sure that all readers of this book would like to stand on the highest point in the south of England — Leith Hill. It just fails (984 ft) to achieve the status of a mountain. But if you ascend the tower you top 1,000 ft and your molehill becomes a mountain. I have never bothered about how many counties I could see with or without field glasses (the record is, I think, thirteen) or whether I could see the Channel through the Shoreham Gap in the South Downs. Sufficient for me is the wide prospect, be it seen through a summer heat or a winter mistiness.

The tower was originally built in 1766 by Richard Hull of Leith Hill Place. Here he is buried feet uppermost they say (but we've heard this kind of legend elsewhere — see Walk 25) so that when the Last Trump is sounded and the world is turned upside down, the Dear Departed, on the mathematical certainty that minus times a minus equals a plus, will positively meet his Maker the right way up.

On the summit is a thatched hut where, at such times as the proprietors judge it worth their while to open, refreshments can be obtained.

Were it not that the few cottages along the short street are built, Surrey-style, of warm red brick instead of being wooden chalets with flowered balconies, we might, at Friday Street, imagine ourselves to be in the depths of the Black Forest or in the Vosges. For here is a delectable lake mirroring tall pines and sturdy oaks.

To reach Friday Street take the A25 out of Dorking in the Guildford direction and in ½ mile or so past the Wotton Hatch Hotel turn leftwards on the Abinger Common road. Ignore, after passing through cuttings, and in 1 mile from the main road, the righthand branch into the village. Keep on for another ⅜ mile and then fork acutely left. The curving road will subsequently bring you to the car park (on the right) for Friday Street.

On leaving the car park at Friday Street, turn rightwards immediately before reaching the road to be on an elevated path which runs parallel to the road below. Subsequently go down steps and continue with the road, very soon to reach the pond at Friday Street. Here turn rightwards (water on left).

You pass the 'Stephen Langton' and where the 'made' road ends,

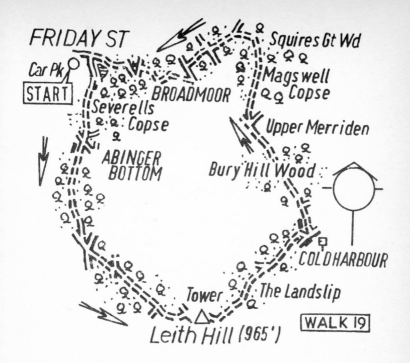

continue ahead by the track through the wood. On reaching a transverse road at Abinger Bottom, turn left. Disregard a left-hand turn which follows. Keep ahead through the wood. You later pass a wire mesh fence on your left ignoring a left-hand path at its corner and subsequently come to a tarmac path with facing sheds.

Here turn right; there is a direction sign for Leith Hill. Follow the path, hedge at first on left, through the wood out to a lane in which turn left. At the road junction soon reached take a clear, signposted bridleway which bisects the angle between Leith Hill road and the Broadmoor road, both signposted.

Now keep straight on, going over any cross-tracks and disregarding any offshoots. The direction is south-east. In about ¾ mile from the road fork just mentioned you come to a wide transverse track with no obvious way ahead.

Turn left here and—quite suddenly—the tower of Leith Hill bursts into view.

Having done honours to the place, stand with your back to the tower, facing the open southward prospect. Now turn left. As a check on this I would say that, if you are coming from the refreshment hut, pass the tower entrance on your left and keep forward.

Over a cross track in a dip you keep forward passing, on your

63

left, the National Trust's 'Duke's Warren' sign. In due course the undulating forward track takes you past the *back* of another NT sign (this on your right) and you come to a wired-off open compound on your left. Another track slants in from the right and you keep forward, now definitely downhill soon to have an almost helicopter view of Coldharbour village below on the right.

So you arrive at the Plough. Opposite this take the public bridleway (signposted), initially past cottages. Just beyond these, at forking paths, take the left-hand one (though, in effect, keeping straight on). You go through the Forestry Commission's Bury Hill woods and, in about ¾ mile from Coldharbour, come to a lonely cottage on the right. It stands in a small clearing. The larger-scale maps name this cottage Upper Merriden Farm (house).

Immediately past the cottage turn rightwards and almost at once fork left on a somewhat stony track which runs northwards through Magswell Copse and Squires Great Wood. At forks, which come in ¼ mile, keep straight on. In a further ¼ mile the track curves leftwards (west) and brings you to a transverse track.

Here turn leftwards (south-west). Maintain this general direction, ignoring any side tracks and going over any cross-tracks (one of them very sandy). The forward way, still generally south-west but winding in places, then narrows and descends—soon quite steeply—and becomes rougher. It takes a leftward bend and you cross a streamlet.

You finally drop to pass Simons Cottage on your left and continue up the drive. A little way along this slant half right on a track. Where this joins a drive continue forward a few yards to meet a road, opposite Home Farm, at Broadmoor.

Turn left for only 100 yards or so. Then, immediately before a notice-board, turn in rightwards, passing on your left a tall wooden gate currently painted green. Quite soon, at a transverse path, turn rightwards. The woodland path rapidly rises to give you a bird's-eye view of the hamlet below. At the next fork bear leftwards.

On coming out to a road cross over and maintain your direction to another lane. Again slant over and maintain the direction. You will soon have the fence of Severells Copse on your left (do not enter the wood—at least, not for the ramble route).

Thus you return to the Friday Street pond again.

Walk 20

Sheepleas and West Horsley Church

3 miles (5 km)

OS sheet 187

Merely going by the name you might imagine Sheepleas to be an extensive area of sheep-dotted pastures. Actually, although there is an enclosed pasture-like tract, the area we visit on this short walk is delightful woodland and is run by the Surrey County Council as a public open space — a very useful buffer indeed, together with common lands, National Trust and Green Belt lands against the subtopian expansion particularly pressing in these parts. Indeed, it is quite possible that on some of the walks in this book, particularly on the outskirts of villages, you may meet some latter-day building development. In such cases the course of the right of way is usually fenced and signposted.

West Horsley church, where a twelfth-century wall painting of St Christopher, patron saint of travellers (even if now demoted somewhat) awaits you, is well worth a visit. The usual guide books have quite a lot to say about its architectural features — many of them very old — and I must refer you to them.

What is unusual, however, is that there is a persistent story, apparently backed by reliable evidence, that the *head* of Sir Walter Raleigh lies buried in a vault beneath the now organ-cluttered St Nicholas chapel. Sir Walter, a towering figure of Elizabeth I's days fell foul of palace politics and was beheaded in 1618 on a trumped-up charge of treason by orders of James I. His *body* was buried either at Beddington in Surrey or in St Margaret's, Westminster. But his severed head is reputedly at West Horsley where his widow and son had residential connections. I don't advise you to start looking for it, however.

The faint hum of traffic on the A246 heard outside the church will bring us back to the second Elizabethan age and to a continuation of our walk.

This walk starts from the car park at Sheepleas. Take the A246 (Guildford) road through, with a double square bend, East Horsley; ¾ mile past the church of West Horsley (on the left) turn leftwards for about a mile. The car park is then met on the left.

Go to the far right-hand corner of the car park (as faced from the entrance). From here a minor track slants half rightwards to join a wider one which runs with an open field just to its right. Very

65

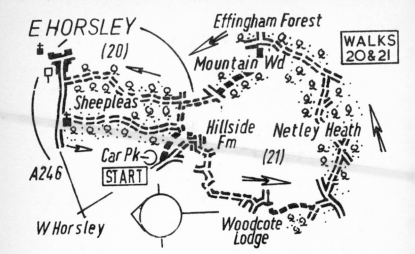

This map covers Walks 20 (circled) and 21

soon bear rightwards and keep rightwards. There should be a small bridleway sign nailed to a tree. The open field just mentioned will be over to your right and you go more or less parallel to it.

The bridleway then becomes much more defined and you come to a T-junction (or, if you count in the minor track ahead, you could say they were cross-tracks). Here turn left.

Now be careful! Sheepleas is a maze of paths and tracks which may change their appearance with conditions of light and their seasonal coverings of fallen leaves. But you cannot go much astray if you keep straight ahead. If you go too far to the right you will run against the boundary of the property. If you go too far left you will come out into an open area, which for this route we do not use.

A detailed description is as follows: Having turned leftwards veer leftwards again at an early fork. Then slant over a cross-track (maintain your direction; don't turn left). The minor track you are on may get a bit indefinite but by maintaining, as just hinted, your forward way you soon join a quite definite track and keep forward in it (a *trifle* leftwards, soon).

The track becomes a hedged bridleway. Do *not*, a little later, enter open country leftwards. Keep on, just inside the edge of the woods. The track now settles down to being a hedged bridleway running through a woodland strip with pleasant fields glimpsed to the left. It passes through a field gate and in due course comes out on the Epsom road (A246). The Duke of Wellington lies just to the right but for the ramble route we turn *leftwards*.

In about ¼ mile we come to West Horsley church (well worth a visit; see introductory notes). Immediately before the church take a bridleway on the left, signposted and with the Surrey CC Open Space insignia. Follow the track, open on left, up to woodland. Here, don't go through the gate ahead but turn rightwards for a few yards. Then turn leftwards through the low barrier and on to a broad track running through a woodlands strip.

Keep straight on over a cross-track. The rising way may be a little hidden by fallen leaves but the direction is never in doubt. A forward track comes in from the right. You then come to an open glade. Make for the far left-hand corner of this. Here you will pick up a clear track through the trees.

In the dip turn right and then, quickly, half right. The car park is then seen ahead.

Though Mountain Wood is rather too ambitious in its name, it certainly is hilly and delightfully wooded. For this is a sylvan region—much of it being Forestry Commission (or similar) territory. There is, however, constant variety both in timber and in type of path, track and driveway. Ramblers who have done other walks in this book will find points of connection and, in fact, some walks could be combined. To avoid confusion, however, I have treated each walk quite separately.

This walk starts from the car park at Sheepleas. See Walk 20 for directions to reach it.

Having parked the car, leave the car park and turn leftwards in the road. Quite soon, after passing a few houses, slant off leftwards on the 'Hillside Farm Private Drive' (so marked). There is, as evinced by the partly foliage-hidden public bridleway sign, a right of way along here.

On reaching the farm turn squarely right. There is a privately-erected footpath sign here. Follow out (noting views to the right) to a road in which turn rightwards. Very soon, at a bend, turn in leftwards on a stony track passing a kennels establishment on your left. At the transverse track, with an electricity pole at the corner, turn rightwards and soon, immediately *before* a field gate opening marked 'Private', turn squarely left on the public bridleway. This stony way brings you to a modern but quite picturesque cluster of farm and estate-type buildings.

Avoid slanting half left here. Disregard, also, a right-hand branch for 'Hookwood'. Keep on, passing a house with a white portico, to a cross-drive or track, the right-hand branch indicated as going to Fullers Farm. Go *over* this transverse way, however, on to a rougher track, obviously well used by horseriders. You pass, at once, a little pond on your left. The bridleway goes round many bends but you cannot go wrong as it is enclosed throughout. At one point, where it may be a bit lush in high summer, it narrows to almost footpath width for a few yards but afterwards becomes wider again.

After going round one rightward bend you come to a pair of new-ish metal field gates. A notice on the forward one cautions you to 'Beware Of The Bull'. Our way, fortunately, lies through the gate on its left and along a little hedged track which you will have seen ahead. It is narrow and enclosed, the type of way in danger of being overgrown. But it seems well used by horse riders and I noted that some encroaching vegetation had been snipped at or swiped at.

I would say, however, that for the greater part of its length the bracken-fringed bridleway was easy going and viable. You come out on a transverse track and turn left, now on a very clear and wider way. This, soon, with a wood on your left brings you out to a road at a little lay-by.

Turn left and, within a few yards, slant off half right on a track of road-like width. On reaching a gate you find, from a sign displayed, that you are entering the Shere Manor Estate's forest lands.

Keep always forward until (with a static water tank facing you) you come to a junction of ways.

Here is a four-way signpost and you turn squarely left for Horsley. Disregard, soon, a minor cross-track. Ignore, also, a left-hand branch a little later. At a transverse track veer rightwards. A little later, just as the track makes a sudden rise, look out for, and take a minor left-hand track, narrow at first but widening later. On my visit I found that owing to logging operations it was in places a bit mauled.

You come out on a firm track or forest road and continue, left, subsequently passing sawmill sheds. A little beyond these you pass through a field gate to a track junction.

Here turn squarely left on what, at first, seems almost a footpath. It rises quite steeply as if Mountain Wood, which you are now about to enter, is trying to justify its name. There will be a plantation fence on your left.

At the top of the rise the bridleway veers rightwards. Whatever the long-term plans for this wood may be, it is, here, currently in its natural state. The track is easily followed and finally runs down-hill out to a lane.

Cross to the drive (Green Dene) opposite but almost at once leave it for the bridleway slanting off to its right. This track is at first quite broad and well used by riders. It then narrows and, quite trimly, brings you to a cross-track.

Here turn left. You soon find you are going not far inland from the left-hand edge of the wood. Continue until you come to a prominent cross-track. Here turn left for a few yards and then slant off half right. The car park is then seen ahead.

It is a moot point whether, in making such a beauty spot as Friday Street the 'object' of your walk, it is better immediately to proceed to it and use it as a base or whether you work your way towards it, building up the pleasurable anticipation.

Users of this book will be able to try both these methods. Walk 19 for example, is based on Friday Street. This one, bound for Friday Street, is based on Westcott — a pleasant village grouped around a small green and with a thatched dovecote for its sign.

The church, perched high and fitting well, it seems, with its surroundings, is one of the earlier works (1832) of Sir George Gilbert Scott.

In the original Rookery House was born, in 1766, Thomas Robert Malthus, author of a much discussed and often misrepresented 'Essay on the Principle of Population' (1798). His theory posited that as population grows in geometrical progression (ie 2, 4, 8, 16 etc), whilst food production grows only in arithmetical progression (ie 1, 2, 3, 4 etc), eventual lack of food would, among other things, damp down the population explosion. Had television been invented in his time, the reverend economist would no doubt have been much in demand as an interviewee or as a panel pundit.

Notes on Friday Street are given in the introduction to Walk 19.

Westcott is on the A25 (Guildford) road just west of Dorking.

As well as pub parking there is some space in the service road between the main road and shops and, discreetly, round the green.

From Westcott village continue in the Guildford road soon to reach the Cricketers. From here, the church is conspicuously seen ahead. Instead of taking the uphill road to it, however, take the elevated path which runs leftwards of, and parallel to, the road, along the edge of the heath. On rejoining the road just past the church slant across and continue, through a line of dwarf posts, by a wide sandy track which runs, parallel to some houses over to the left, out to a minor transverse road.

Cross this to a tarmac drive which soon ends at a 'banjo' parking place (private). Veer a little left of this and continue by the downhill, narrow track, soon passing sandhills on your right.

Thus you re-reach the Guildford road. After turning left for a

few yards, turn squarely left in the stony Rookery drive. Subsequently go round a rightward bend, crossing the Pipp Brook. Note the mill waterfall on the left.

On coming to the re-developed Rookery disregard the forward drive. Instead, fork left on an enclosed path, passing the Georgian-style terrace on your right. Via an iron gate you come to a wooden field gate. At this point slant off half right through wooden posts and follow the path between wire fencing quite steeply up through the woods, out to a transverse track.

Here turn left. The way is quite sunken. Note, for easier progress, parallel paths on the right. So you continue with a wood on your left. Don't enter it.

Just after the wood ends disregard a path on the left (but note the view). Soon after this look for, and take, a path on the right which runs with a wood on the left and wire on the right out to a cross-track. Here turn left.

Quite soon take a path on the right.

(Before turning over this stile, however, it is worth continuing for rather over ¼ mile more. Then, if you look for it, you will see a pretty little waterfall on the left. Return and continue with the main ramble, ie from the stile originally on the right though it will, of course, now be on the left as you return.)

It runs down between two pools and then up to a stile. Over this there is a right-left bend and a path which runs steeply uphill through a wood with, initially, wire fencing on the right and then wire on both sides. By a stile you reach a lane and cross to a stile opposite.

Ignore a right-hand branch and also a left-hand one which immediately follows. A little later turn leftwards on a transverse track to (at Kempslade Farm) a stile by a wooden field gate. Here turn rightwards in the tarmac drive. It then runs into a lane which comes in from the left and so you reach Friday Street pond.

You may well wish to look around and possibly to visit the 'Stephen Langton' inn (for this, skirt the pond on your left). For the ramble route, however, note that immediately on reaching the pond, you turn left, pond on right, on a track/path.

This soon veers away from the pond and has an old fence over to the right. A little later, avoid (possibly beguiled by the National Trust sign) going rightwards into Severells Copse. Instead, *keep straight on* (and rising).

On coming out on a lane, with a signpost visible to the right, slant over to the opposite track, cutting a road corner. On soon crossing another lane, keep, at first, forward. Then veer rightwards. You subsequently have an elevated view of the hamlet of Broadmoor. By taking, later, a path on the left you come out, by garage-shed doors, to a lane at Broadmoor. Here turn left for about 100 yards.

Opposite Home Farm go up a drive ('Bridle Path Only'). In a few yards at an iron post which once supported a 'bridleway' sign, fork off half-left. On coming to a drive turn left soon to pass a house (Simons Cottage) on your right.

The ensuing track is, at first, narrow, rutted and steep. You cross a little upland stream, which supplies the waterfall previously mentioned, and bear rightwards. After going over a cross-track the way levels out and becomes wider. You pass a gate and adjacent stile and come out on one of the most sandy tracks you'll ever expect to find in a lifetime of country walking.

Cross directly over. Ignore, almost at once, a minor left-hand offshoot and a little later similarly disregard a right-hand branch. Then ignore an intriguing ride on the left. You may be tempted to detour along this. The view, at the end, whilst pleasant, cannot compare with that which you will see in a couple of minutes' time.

Keep on, therefore, to reach a track junction — with good views over to the Ranmore Common heights. Disregard a track going squarely left. Also disregard the wide track forward. Between these you will find another (half-left) track. Go down it. Your landmark will be a white chalk scar in the hills ahead. As so often happens in this area, the track here is stony but, as again is usually the case, gives way to sand.

Keep straight on, ignoring a right-hand offshoot. An enclosed sandy track brings you to a large house on the right. Here bear half right (follow the hoof-prints!) between the houses and stables of Squires Farm. Then follow the 'made' drive out to a road.

Immediately opposite is a stile and footpath signpost. From this proceed forward over the grass and then passing a wood on your immediate left. Beyond this continue forward aiming for the left-hand end of the farm seen ahead. Here you join a farm road and turn left in it. The enclosed part ends at a white-painted metal field gate. From here the technical line of the bridleway is a gradual slant over to the hedge on the left-hand side of the meadow. You might find it more convenient (and more helpful to the farmer in mowing time) if you continued forward with the wire fence on your right and at the meadow end turned left a few yards to join the bridleway.

Keep always forward in this, soon with a little brook for company, to come out at a lanehead. The woodland strip you have just traversed has concealed a lake on the right. If you have come at the right day and time, as indicated by the notice boards displayed, you can, on joining the lanehead just mentioned, detour rightwards to view this lake.

For the ramble route, however, keep ahead to the charming hamlet of Milton Street. Here cross (leftwards) the brook by the footbridge with wooden guardrails. Continue forward on the grassy track, soon narrowing and rising. Go over a cross-track.

Garden fencing now starts. Look out, soon, for a branch path on the right. This, enclosed, runs down, with a left-right bend, to a lanehead. Here keep forward, past the school, to the main road. Here turn left (on the sidewalk) very soon to reach Westcott centre.

Walk 23

Norbury Park and Fetcham Downs

6½ miles (9.5 km)

OS sheet 187

When all is so comparatively rural and peaceful hereabouts one wonders how Roaringhouse Farm got its name. Was it ever the scene of some rural industry necessitating a roaring forge and stentorian bellows?

Norbury Park (also met with in Walk 17) is reputedly one of the finest in Surrey. After changing hands with considerable frequency most of it was finally acquired, for public enjoyment, by the Surrey County Council in the mid thirties and so saved from the fate of being cut up into building plots.

The railway from Leatherhead to Dorking runs through and in one place penetrates part of the estate. The line and its tunnel entrances (seen on this walk) seem quite interesting but there was a furore when the line was first mooted. John Stuart Mill, a local resident, strenuously protested. He failed to stop the railway engineers. But the railway engineers did not quench the famous philosopher-economist's crusading zeal. He subsequently became a founder of the Commons Preservation Society, as it was originally named, and was very active in it.

This walk starts from Burford Bridge. Through Leatherhead take the Dorking road (which now bypasses Mickleham). Just before reaching the Burford Bridge Hotel you will not fail to notice a large public car park.

From the car park at Burford Bridge turn back in the Dorking direction passing the white-fronted inn, once the Fox and Hounds. (Lord Nelson spent his last night ashore here before Trafalgar.) Keep to the left-hand side of the main road quite soon to reach the pedestrian subway. Cross over and on emerging go along the lane passing the Stepping Stones inn and, a little later, Boxhill railway station.

Immediately over the railway bridge turn rightwards on a path at first enclosed and then running by the embankment. The Mole is then crossed by an iron bridge. A little beyond this the track/path bends clearly half left to a house (Cowslip Cottage) seen ahead. Pass this on your left and continue up the drive. A few yards before this turns squarely right (at Cowslip farm), turn squarely *left* opposite a brick shed on a concreted track with a hedge on the right.

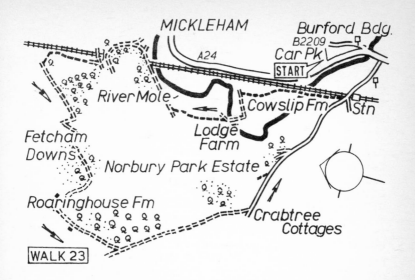

This soon turns squarely rightwards and takes you over the Mole again. Immediately before reaching Lodge Farm (ahead) shift to the left so that, whilst maintaining your forward direction, you pass the rear of the farm on your immediate right — now by a grassy track.

Continue, always ahead (later ignore a right-hand branch) by various stiles and through pleasant meadows until, after rising a little, you come to a track/drive and turn rightwards in it. You soon pass above the entrance to the railway tunnel and then come to a transverse drive. Cross this and go over the grass opposite to join another drive in which turn left.

As this goes round a leftward curve you will see a line of a dozen posts on the right with a path starting between them. *Disregard this.* In only a few yards farther, however, turn rightwards on a path down through the trees to, and over, a cross-track and then up again to a stile by a gate.

You come out on an elevated open area. There are no marked paths but slant very slightly rightwards, soon steeply downhill to a stile by a field gate just to the right of a small wood.

Over this stile turn left on a grass track with the wood on your left and the railway to your right. (As the trains go by they seem, from this viewpoint, like models on a table top or floor.)

Before very long look carefully for a V 'stile' (a real fat man's agony!). Over or through this you will find a path — a slight detour to skirt a fallen tree — which gives on to the main, enclosed track. This, rising, runs immediately outside the north-west side of the open area you have just been in.

A wood then starts on your left and the track levels out. Note, at this point, a fine view over to the right.

Continue in the track until your forward way is halted by a Private Woodlands sign. At this point turn squarely right. Now be careful. Before long you enter woodlands and pass, first, a multi-stemmed old yew on your right and then a smaller, single-stemmed one. Opposite this latter turn left. The path, through trees, is almost a mini-track and quite clear once you have located the start.

At an old log seat the path bends squarely right and soon bends squarely left. As it is enclosed you have no chance of going astray. It finally runs out on a broad grassy bridleway in which you keep left. The track, rising slightly (this is the Fetcham Downs area), has log seats for the weary or the contemplative.

When the open area on the right ends, the track, now curving a little leftwards, runs between bushes. Very soon a track slants in acutely from the right. Here turn V-wise right almost doubling on your tracks. Follow out this track, soon past some magnificent wide-spreading beeches downhill and out to a transverse track in which turn rightwards soon to reach Roaringhouse Farm.

Here turn squarely left on a rough little lane (do not turn acutely left into the woods) soon passing a farm on the right. Disregard a right-hand track and continue ahead with a wood on your left and a vast field on your right. At the end of the latter continue ahead (the bridleway now being enclosed) and follow it all the way (somewhat over a mile from Roaringhouse Farm) to a little cross-road at Crabtree Cottages.

Here turn left. The way with lovely views is drive-like and down-hill and continues so to Boxhill station. Here retrace a little of your outward way to the car park.

Walk 24

Burford Bridge and Box Hill

4 miles (6.5 km)

OS sheet 187

Box Hill has strong claims to being the most famous viewpoint in the whole of England. Other hills may be much higher. Box Hill barely exceeds 600 ft and although you can motor nearly to the top you can reach the summit excitingly by a choice of precipitous paths and tracks. This walk indicates one way up. See Walk 25 for another.

Box Hill is named from its fine box trees though many other species — whitebeam, oak, beech, yews and junipers, for example, add to its beauty and make for variety throughout the year.

Whilst the hill owes a lot of its eclat to being so near London and so easily accessible, it is obvious that, in the final analysis, it is the character of the view which really counts. And connoisseurs of countryside charm all agree that at Box Hill the downland scenery is of the highest quality.

There is no need for me, here, to list even the chief of the points, near and far, to be observed from the summit on a fine day. For here, incorporated into a stone memorial breast work is a view indicator — a bit weathered and not without its graffiti, but still very informative.

Despite its accessibility and popularity Box Hill summit does not seem grossly vulgarized. There is plenty of room for all. And on this walk you soon get away from any hamburger munching, cola clutching school kids to penetrate 'lonely woods with paths dim and silent'.

This walk starts from Burford Bridge, the directions to which are given for Walk 23.

From the car park at Burford Bridge turn back in the Dorking direction, past the white-fronted hotel (formerly the Fox and Hounds) keeping to the left-hand side of the main road. Quite soon — just after crossing the bridge over the Mole and immediately before the start of the pedestrian subway ramp — turn left on a short spur of hedged track which brings you to a stile with a little iron ladder.

Here you join the Mole and have this on your left as you follow the curving riverside path under the steep slopes of Box Hill. So you come to the green-painted iron footbridge erected by the Ramblers' Association as a memorial to its members who fell in

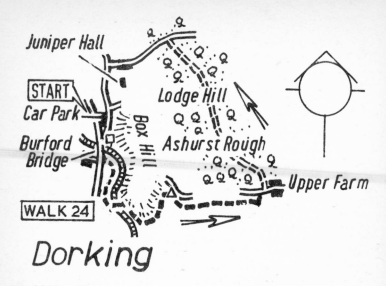

Juniper Hall

START
Car Park

Burford
Bridge

Box Hill

Lodge Hill

Ashurst Rough

Upper Farm

WALK 24

Dorking

World War II.

You can, and especially if the river is in flood and running strongly, cross here. Then turn rightwards, river on right, to reach a prominent cross-track just above the Stepping Stones. Here turn left.

But, alternatively, instead of crossing by the bridge you can continue by the river a little longer to come to the hexagonal Stepping Stones. (More fun to cross these than by the bridge!) Over the stones, keep forward, past, currently, a large tree stump.

Either way, continue by the wide track with a boundary fence on your right. You will notice, on a post, a blue waymark. Look out for these. The track soon veers rightwards and starts to rise in real earnest. At the next fork veer leftwards, don't descend. Note the blue waymarks. At the top of the rise turn rightwards on the obviously more-used path, ignoring a minor left offshoot. The path may be masked, at one point, by a fallen tree around which you detour.

The path, having levelled off for a while, rises slowly. So you come out on an upland open area. Here turn squarely left although, if you find the ensuing gradient too steep, you could lessen it by going half-left. The square-left way would appear better, however, as, whilst the path is not too 'worn', there are little footholds which you will find of great practical use.

Take it slowly and steadily enjoying, during pauses, the fine view over to Dorking and beyond. At the top you will find a very clear path/track in which you turn rightwards. So you reach the summit of Box Hill.

If you require the Old Fort tea rooms — or rather the smaller establishment that has replaced them — turn acutely left (there is a sign board indicating the way) to reach the road and follow this round to the left, past the car park.

For the main ramble route pass the summit memorial on your immediate left and keep on, parallel with the view, by what, at first, is a well marked track. When this suddenly ends, maintain the direction over the grass, taking care not to lose height.

Eventually woodland approaches from the right and a wall of green faces you. At this point turn leftwards and, at the belt of trees, go half right to reach the road in which turn rightwards. Quite soon you come to the Upper Farm caravan site and its 'leisure' amenities. There is a snack bar adjacent.

Immediately before these, turn leftwards on a bridleway, with the caravan site fence at first on your immediate right. Disregard an opening to the left. The track then takes a *very slight* leftwards trend and descends slightly. At the next fork take care to go left, uphill. You pass, on your right, a wired-off clearing (a new plantation possibly).

At the cross-track turn rightwards with another side of the wired-off clearing on your right. Now keep absolutely straight on. The track, through yew and juniper (among other trees) is quite well marked and the general direction, if you carry a pocket compass — always a useful asset in forest walks — is north-north-west. The track descends very slowly.

On my visit I found, later, a fallen beech in process of being sawn up athwart the track, calling for a detour round it. It may well be that when you come this way the debris has been cleared though the gap may remain. The track, however, keeps forward, now narrower and definitely descending. You come out on a white track running through a wooded valley. Here one might well imagine oneself to be in the Ardennes, the Vosges, the Black Forest — not in Surrey.

Turn left in the track. It soon becomes hedged and runs out into a lane. Here turn left. At the transverse road turn left and so (past Juniper Hall) back to your starting point.

Walk 25   Box Hill and Juniper Top

3½ miles (5.5 km)

OS sheet 187

This walk, whilst covering the same area as 24, goes over different paths. There was so much of interest that it could not be confined to *one* walk. Hence this second ramble over Box Hill. As with the first it is based on the car park at Burford Bridge.

From the car park at Burford Bridge turn back in the Dorking direction and very soon, immediately before the hotel, turn left up the hill.

The way is obvious — up! It is fairly steep but as you take (as I imagine) frequent rests, you will be delighted with your progress as the panorama unfolds. The car park you so recently started from soon seems a long way below.

There will be trees on your right. Subsequently you arrive at a broad chalk track, here as wide as a road. Turn rightwards in it. Though you still continue to rise, the stiff climbing has now been done.

You enter a copse and pass, on your immediate left, the memorial stone, seemingly fairly new, to the eccentric Dorking man who in the year 1800 was here buried upside down. There were many, in those days, who seriously believed that, when Judgement Day came, the world would be literally turned upside down. Thus, if one were interred upside down one would then, again reversed, meet one's Maker the right way up! (See, also, notes to Walk 19.)

Being glad to be alive and in normal vertical position we continue, avoiding a rightward slant, out to a road opposite the hill-top car park. The Old Fort tea rooms (or rather the hut now replacing them) lie just to the left. For the ramble route turn *rightwards*. The summit memorial-cum-view indicator is then seen half right ahead. We pass this on our immediate left and continue by a track.

When this comes to an end, we continue, over the grass, in the same direction taking care not to lose height. Trees come up from the right and eventually there is a 'bay' of trees ahead. At (or near) here, turn leftwards uphill soon to reach the belt of trees. Slant half rightwards through these to a road in which turn rightwards. You soon come to a group of buildings comprising the Upper Farm 'Leisure Park' and snack bar.

Here, at the '30' sign and immediately before a barn with a 'tin'

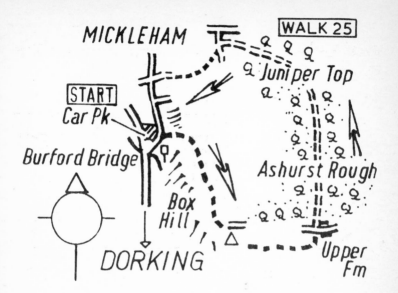

roof, turn leftwards. In a few yards you will be on a clear bridleway (indicated as a horse track). There will be the fence of the caravan site on your right. Where this fence ends continue ahead, past a beech tree and soon going leftwards at a fork, ignoring any minor branches.

We then come to a prominent yew. Immediately *before* this is a right-hand track which we disregard. Immediately *past* this is another right-hand track which we also disregard. *Ahead*, however, are two forking paths of which we take the rightmost, downhill. In about 200 yards along this stony way look out for a path branching off half right. Except for one or two places where we may have, in high summer, to brush aside (easily) encroaching greenery (experienced walkers who often pack a pair of secateurs in their rucksack or who are able to give a swipe or two with a walking stick—please note) the path is a good one and brings us out into the open with a delightful view across the valley (Juniper Bottom) below.

The path then re-enters woodland. At one point it widens but a little later you may wonder whether you have lost it for a carpet of fallen leaves covers the ground. But not to worry! Just keep forward in line with the valley. You won't, in these woods, now be able to see it but you will recall its direction. Whenever there is any doubt, go half rightwards through the trees upwards and you will strike a clear track. Here turn left to come out on an open hillside — Juniper Top — with glorious views towards Mickleham Downs (see Walk 26) ahead and Ranmore Common (see Walk 16) over to the left. You are approximately 550 ft up.

Keep along the centre of this open area, slowly descending. At its end it becomes a woodland track and we soon come to a spot, with a road a little to the right, where a hedged track slants in from the left. Here turn acutely left almost doubling on our tracks.

In a short ¼ mile we come to open grass slopes with a birch clump with seven (I think) branches immediately ahead. At this point *turn back*. In about 45 steps you will find a path now on your left. Take this. After a coy start it becomes clear — and steep. (NB The path you should be on runs *through* woodland. If you have a wood on your right and an open slope on the left you are not on the correct path!)

Soon you have a paling fence on your right, marking the boundary of the National Trust property. At the top the path becomes a track veering rightwards. Terrace-like it soon gives a delightful view of Juniper Hall rightwards and below.

It then becomes a rough drive and curves downhill (take care here) to the road. Here turn leftwards, back, in ¼ mile, to the car park at Burford Bridge.

Box Hill was once named White Hill (from its chalk) but White Hill is the name now given to Box Hill's near neighbour and one which we visit on this walk. It includes a rural section of the old Roman Stane Street, which connected London and Chichester. Most of this walk is over the yew-clad Mickleham Downs, and has the feature that most of the ascent is done at one burst not long after the start. This done, one can enjoy the rest of the walk at leisure.

This walk is again based on the Burford Bridge car park, the directions to which are given in Walk 23.

From the car park at Burford Bridge proceed Londonwards, disregarding, at the foot of the Box Hill slopes, the little right-hand turning. Continue past Juniper Hall (note the signboard outside) and soon after turn rightwards. In about ¾ mile you come, on the right, to a hedged bridleway. *Opposite* this you will find a gap with a track (an old fence on its left) going very steeply uphill.

Here you must gird up your loins and make the ascent. Do it slowly and *carefully*, especially if the chalk is at all slippery after rain. I am young metaphorically in heart only but found no special difficulty though I used my walking stick in the manner of an alpenstock. But it is little adventures like this (and, for example, the crossing of the Mole by the Stepping Stones on Walk 24) which make country walking *interesting*.

May I repeat—take care here. Sliding down the slope to the lane below would *not* be funny.

The track then veers rightwards north-east and, levelling out, becomes a neat way between trees. You come (this is White Hill) to a seat and a wonderful view over to the Box Hill woodlands.

At the fork here, go left with an old fence on your left. At an angle of this turn left and, in a few yards, slant off half right on the obvious track north-east. 'Daylight' is seen over to the left. The track starts to rise a little and, later, a track slants in from the right.

On coming to a definite cross-track turn left, with an old fence reinforced with some new wire on your right. On coming to another prominent (and wide) cross-track turn rightwards with wire on the left and a paling fence on the right. As you turn, there is a wooden gate on the corner (right).

Follow this clear bridleway. There are fascinating peeps of open country to the right. One wishes that, at intervals, there could be openings, or 'windows', cut. There is then woodland on the right. Just before the track comes out, at posts, to a road, and at a public bridleway signpost (point Z), turn acutely left.

The M25 is planned to come this way but is not likely to affect very much the bridleway junction at point Z.

There are some lovely views, rightwards, over the golf course. The pounded bridleway (with, in many places, a way along the edge for pedestrians) becomes almost a leafy tunnel. A clearing destined for a new plantation is passed on the left. Just after entering a bit of 'old' woodland one finds a prominent crosstrack. Here turn left. You will be on the course of a Roman Road—Stane Street.

The way, except for one momentary constriction, is quite wide and clear. You reach a valley track with a gate leading into the new plantation on your left. Keep ahead, however, up a sharp short rise. Then bear half right south-west with, at first, a conifer plantation on the left.

You then reach a clearing. Keep forward; don't bear half right. Keep forward along the right-hand side of the clearing with trees on your right. Where the trees and a path veer rightwards to a concrete pedestal (an OS Triangulation mark) *keep forward* over the grass to enter woodland again. A minor path slants in from the right and you go along a slightly left bend, downhill a little, to pass a National Trust 'Mickleham Downs' plaque.

Immediately past this ignore a half-right fork. The track, fairly wide, runs straight through a wood. You pass through, or by, an iron gate. You go under a bridge carrying an overhead drive and finally out on a lane. Here turn rightwards for a few yards and then turn leftwards, past Juniper Hall and so back to the Burford Bridge car park again.

Walk 27

6 miles (9.5 km)

OS sheet 187

The Buckland Hills

The plan of this walk is very simple. Starting from the summit of Reigate Hill we walk westwards — mainly over National Trust properties — but pleasantly by rights of way through some private ones — along the top of the Downs. We go over Colley Hill (756 ft) the magnificent view from which was extolled by William Cobbett (1762-1835) in his *Rural Rides*. It must not be imagined that he was impressed by 'scenery' as we — mostly a nation of townsmen — now regard it. He wrote that Hindhead (see Walk 2) was 'certainly the most villainous spot that God had ever made'. He was an agriculturalist concerned with the farming aspects and as we survey the entrancing view the Weald certainly seems fruitful.

After going along the top of the well-wooded Buckland Hills we return, by a parallel course, below them.

As you come off the open hillside of Colley Hill and enter a little byway you will notice, on the right, a little way down, an iron 'coal post'. A hundred or so years ago the Corporation of London levied a tax on all coal entering the metropolis and, to mark the limits of the area involved, a large number of 'coal posts' were set up. The tax was later dropped but a large number of the posts remain. You may well come across others in your rambles round London.

The walk starts from the top of Reigate Hill. One possible approach would be by the A217 via Banstead. Just past Lower Kingswood you come to the roundabout where the M25 runs in. Continue down the hill but in only ¼ mile where a couple of minor roads V-off on the left, you will find the car park.

From the car park make for the footbridge in view which spans the main road and continue rising by the tree-shaded stony drive. You go over a cross-drive, pass a few cottages on the left and a water tower and radio mast on the right and in about ¾ mile emerge on the open slopes of Colley Hill (there is a National Trust sign) by an ornate but now non-functioning memorial fountain.

Half left ahead the slopes of Leith Hill are seen. Reigate itself is mainly screened by trees.

Continue forward by the right-hand trees. Where the horse track veers a little rightwards, at a line of posts, veer off slightly left on a grassy track, soon through a clump of trees. Now keep this direction,

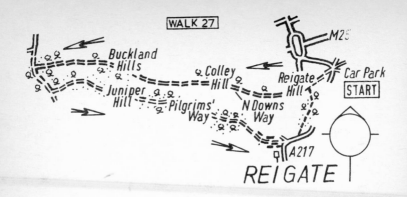

ie along the open hill top, near the right-hand woodland. A line of seats marks the way and you pass a water tower over to the right. A deep coombe is passed on the left.

You subsequently come to a spot where a wood immediately ahead marks the end of the open access area. Here, at a NT sign, you rejoin the horseriders' way, actually a trackway of considerable antiquity, and find yourself now going forward on a little enclosed byway. On soon reaching a fork with horse-barriers take the left-most branch (ie keep straight on) and follow it out to a tarmac drive.

Here turn left but for only a few yards. Immediately after passing a house and adjacent drive on the left and immediately before coming to a private drive on the right, turn rightwards on an enclosed path. Follow this out to where (at 'Mount Hill' gates) a gravelled drive slants across. Here maintain your forward direction soon passing 'The Bounty' and 'Little Gables' on your right.

Housing (which hasn't been too obtrusive) tails off and you find yourself going through a wood. After much rain you may be glad to detour on any side paths you can find. But as this is a legal *bridleway* we must share it—cheerfully, I hope—with our fellow outdoor folk, the horse riders.

On emerging from the wood, a fine and extensive view greets the eye. You continue by a fenced path (wood on right). The path then bends squarely left (downhill) and, quite soon, squarely right round the fenced-off field. At the field end it bends rightwards and up-wards but then slants off to the left through the woods, soon bearing rightwards. At a further fork turn rightwards to reach, in a few yards, a fairly wide bridleway.

Turn left in this. It subsequently curves rightwards. As it comes into the straight (as the racing commentators say) with a cottage ahead along an avenue, look for an acutely left turning and take it, almost doubling on your tracks on a rough and 'hollow' way which drops down between weird yews. Keep on, disregarding any off-shoots until the wood on your right ends and there is a distinct fenced gap on the right. Don't confuse this with a *woodland* gap met earlier on; one which has, on the other side of the main track, a large chalk pit.

Now retrace your way for about 50 steps — normal ones, not giant strides! Then take (it will now be on your right though, of course, leftwards from your first approach) an uphill path/mini-track. It is quite steep and, in wet weather, slippery but in only a few yards it levels out and runs, with a wonderful view of the Buckland Hills, with a wire fence on the right and very soon bends rightwards.

Now for the next couple of miles or so, the basic route instruction can be summed up very simply: Keep along the foot of the hills with the wire fence always to, or closely parallel to, your right.

You will be going along the Pilgrims Way. On the whole the going varying from path to track is quite clear and only very occasionally did I find a spot where a swipe with a walking stick or a snip from secateurs would have done some good. Your way is varied by going through groves of ancient yews. Chalk-loving wild flowers abound in summer.

So you come to a National Trust 'Juniper Hill' sign. Keep always ahead. The direction is generally east so you'll have the sun behind you and your shadow before.

The way now curves between yews and at one point runs down steps. Impossible to describe every minor offshoot but at a conspicuous cross-track avoid slanting rightwards. You finally go forward alongside a large field (paddock?) with white fencing and come out on a lane end where, over a few yards of gravel, the tarmac starts and housing begins.

Go forward but at an early fork bear left (for 'Underbeeches') and in a matter of a few yards turn rightwards on an enclosed alleyway ('No Through Way' and with a bridleway sign). This runs between walls and fencing out to the main road near the top of Reigate Hill.

Just to the right is the Yew Tree. It could be that the Sir Galahad of the party could leave other members here whilst he pushed on ahead — and up! — to fetch the car. But for the final lap, turn left in the main road!

In only a few yards — after passing house no 117 and a private drive for 'Verwood' on the left — slant half left on a wooded path. This is quite easily missed. In a few yards you will find a rather elderly signpost bearing the legend 'Public Highway'. Of course, footpaths are as much 'highways' as M-roads are but this is the first time I've seen a footpath so described on a signpost. More to the point, however, is why this sign is not at the *beginning* of the path. It may be shifted by the time you come this way.

This uphill path runs into the avenue by which you first started the walk and here you turn rightwards back to the car park.

Walk 28   Marden Park and South Hawke

8 miles (13 km)

OS sheet 187

A casual glance at a 1:50,000 OS map might give the impression
that Croydon's commuter-land countryside is well peppered with
villa-residences and any walk in this area would be semi-suburban.

The flood of housing which, before World War II, gave the
impression that Surrey was one vast building site has now been
checked and controlled by Green Belt policies.

The lovely hill and dale country we traverse today is still sur-
prisingly rural and where any residential roads have to be traversed,
you will find that they are quite pleasant and not very long.

The chief feature of this walk is the National Trust viewpoint at
South Hawke and the other viewpoint above the Oxted lime works.

Just a word about the distance, bearing in mind that this is quite
an up-and-down walk. I asked a mixed party, of varying ages and
containing no-one who could be called an experienced walker, to
test this route I had planned. They did it without undue effort
between eleven and four on a mid-January day. Admittedly their
picnic lunchtime at South Hawke was not extended. In fairer
weather they would have lingered much longer.

There are, by the way, no inns directly on this route so, as just
hinted, a picnic lunch is indicated.

The start is from the car park at Woldingham railway station.
Take the A22 and at the roundabout not long after passing
Whyteleafe South station turn left and, at the crossroads just past
the railway viaduct, turn rightwards.

There is a pay car park at Woldingham station. But I did not,
on my visit, see any notices prohibiting discreet parking in Church
Road adjacent.

On leaving the car park at Woldingham station turn sharp right
in Church Road with the railway on your right. In a short ¼ mile
turn rightwards over the railway bridge and then bear left.

Now keep straight on, disregarding the rightward branch into the
yard of Marden Park Farm. The rising track, becoming rougher, is
followed out until, after about 1¼ miles it becomes tamed into a
forward drive and Roehampton Park School (for girl boarders) —
so named because it was moved here from Roehampton near
Richmond — comes into view.

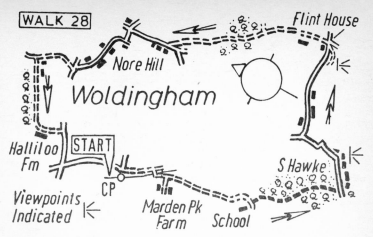

WALK 28
Flint House
Nore Hill
Woldingham
Halliloo Fm
START
S Hawke
Viewpoints Indicated
CP
Marden Pk Farm
School

Disregard a drive on the left. Pass, on your left, a splendid tall clipped topiary hedge and at its corner cross a drive to a stile opposite.

Now ascend the long ridge, with a line of trees on your left, up to a stile in an angle of fencing. The ensuing path through the wood is, initially, quite clear. Soon, however, owing to a carpet of leaves, fallen trees and a number of alternative paths made by horseriders (who, having pulped up one path proceed to mar another) the way ahead may seem vague.

Not to worry in the least! The true path is never more than 100 yards from the right-hand side of the wood and is often less. Bearing this in mind and keeping forward, you reach, in a short ½ mile from the stile just mentioned, a little lane.

Here turn left. There is no *need* to keep to the road as there are parallel paths to the right. In any case you will soon see seats over to the right. Here is the South Hawke viewpoint, over 750 ft up.

Continue in the road, round bends and past the car park. You will be going along Gangers Hill with, on the left, extensive views over Marden Park. At the road junction then reached bear right-wards along The Ridge (part residential but elegantly so).

In about ½ mile a lay-by will be seen on the right (another possible car park). The rather formidable wire fencing here is to prevent others suffering the sad fate of Eileen Dover. For you are immediately and precipitously above the Greystone Lime Works. These may not be the acme of beauty, but the view over the Weald (for you are 868 ft up) is very fine. Southward there is the green-sand range from Toys Hill to Leith Hill and beyond these, the ridges of the Weald climaxing in Ashdown Forest. And beyond these if you are the guide-book writers' blue-eyed boy, you can see the South Downs. On an exceptionally clear day you can, I read, even see the Chilterns to the north-west.

Continue, by the fence, in the little lane which ensues. To avoid an extremely muddy patch just before it runs out to The Ridge go through a hedge gap on the left and then turn rightwards in the road very soon to come to a road junction. Here, by the side of Flint House, turn left on a bridleway signposted to Warlingham.

At the arched entrance to 'Whistlers Wood' house keep straight on (No Through Road sign). You subsequently pass, over to your right, what I presume is an aircraft beacon or a radar station.

Now for the first time since leaving Woldingham car park you start descending and will probably have to detour (no special trouble) round hoof-pulped mud patches. You emerge in an open field and keep forward, at first by a bit of hedge and then as an unploughed strip over downland.

As you reach the far side it would seem that your way is along a short clear track. Not so. Technically, at any rate, you go a little rightwards of this making for a public bridleway signpost seen in the hedge.

Either way, turn rightwards in the lane which, on its left, is lined with some smart newish houses. You are on the eastern outskirts of Woldingham.

In a short ½ mile, where the lane which has been descending now starts to rise, turn left in Upland Road opposite Warren Barn Farm. Quite soon turn rightwards in the transverse road and follow it out to the transverse Slines New Road. Here turn left but in only a couple of dozen yards or so, turn rightwards on a track—High Lane and so marked.

You quite soon reach a valley bottom and then climb out of it by ensuing chalky, hedged track. Just after passing 'High Leas' house on the left, turn left in Plantation Lane (so marked). It is actually a bridleway running along the top edge of the lovely valley which you have just crossed. Follow this out, later curving leftwards downhill, through Halliloo Farm which has been seen ahead and along the concrete-slab farm road, out to a transverse road.

Here turn rightwards. At the crossroads turn left to reach Woldingham station and its car park again.

Walk 29   South Hawke and Winders Hill

4 miles (6.5 km)

OS sheet 187

Here is quite a short walk based on the National Trust car park of South Hawke. It has an advantage that it is mostly over firm drives and a little lane. For ½ mile through the woods, however, it is another matter. I think that the National Trust and/or the Surrey County Council should provide a proper horse riders' track here; rubble based and gravel topped. Few horse riders would deign to use it, but walkers would! This woodland section repeats, though in the reverse direction, a small bit of Walk 28.

To arrive at the start of this walk first follow the directions in Walk 28 to Woldingham station. Opposite Woldingham station take the road which, soon curving rightwards, takes you past the church (built 1933 to replace the previous very tiny one; evidence of the village's growth). Keep straight on, subsequently with a golf course on your left. At a T-junction, turn rightwards along Gangers Hill. You will soon find the car park on the right. But watch for it since, as a general policy, car parks in such a situation are deliberately made inconspicuous and signery is not allowed to mar scenery. After parking you continue in the road.

On leaving the car park at South Hawke turn rightwards in the road passing, on the left, the seats which mark the viewpoint. In a trifle over ¼ mile — just before reaching a fork — turn rightwards on a signposted footpath.

It could happen that before very long you will find that the strict theoretical path through the wood is confused by various divergencies but this should not bother you in the least if you note that at no time does the path run more than 100 yards from the left-hand edge of the wood, and for much of the time it is nearer. At its end, ½ mile from the road, it runs almost against the left-hand edge and you come to a stile.

Here continue downhill with a line of trees on your right to reach another stile. Over this turn left in the drive and in a matter of yards, *squarely left* again. (If you find yourself passing the school and the convent you have taken the wrong direction!)

You should be on an avenue which, in ¾ mile, meets, at Winders Hill, the transverse North Downs Way. Here turn left. In just over ¼ mile you come to a fork.

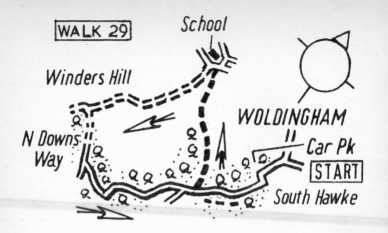

Here take the left branch and follow the little wooded lane, soon round a square left-right bend, back to the car park at South Hawke. There is no need to keep to the road all the time. Make some ad-lib exploration of the parallel paths and tracks to the right.

Walk 30

7 miles (11 km)

Bletchingley and Godstone

OS sheet 187

Both Bletchingley (sometimes spelled without the first 't') and Godstone are delightful villages, the latter having a fine green and some attractive inns at one of which William Cobbett (see also Walk 27) stopped on one of his *Rural Rides* and ate his bread and cheese. In the churchyard lies buried beneath a sarsen stone set up by the London rambling clubs, 'Walker Miles' (S. F. Taylor, 1853-1908), a pioneer writer on rambling in south-east England. I dearly wish, as a later, fellow practitioner, I had some of his published writings (and that's a hint for any reader who could help me). Certain it is that most — or even all — of the paths we use today were described by him in those days of Norfolk jackets and knickerbockers and of Edwardian skirts which set off a trimly booted ankle as the ladies were helped over stiles.

Walkingstead, by the way, is the name of the area around Leigh Place near Godstone. *Stead* (a place or site) is a common place-name element. The *Walking* probably derives from a personal name.

Bletchingley is on the A25. As this is a circular walk it could alternatively be started, if more convenient, from Godstone (on the A22).

There is a small public car park at Godstone but parking may be easier at Bletchingley. The main street is wide and there are car parking spaces between the roadway and the shops.

According to where you have parked, there are two options in starting out from Bletchingley:

(a) From the Whyte Harte walk (westwards) up the High Street for about 300 yards until a side road appears on the left, with an antiques shop at the corner. Take this turning. Within 100 yards, at a gateway in front, two footpaths are signposted, left and right. Take the tarmac path on the left, running beside a house. On reaching the road turn rightwards to the signed entry to the Aggregate Company's Works on the left.

(b) From the crossroads at the eastern end of the High Street take the minor road southwards for a short ¼ mile to the works entrance above-mentioned.

Either way Follow the concrete quarry road, passing a pond on the left. Where (soon) tall trees appear on the right, and where

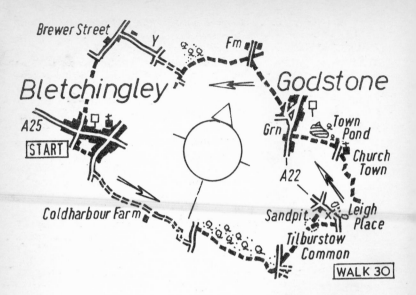

Map labels: Brewer Street, Y, Fm, Bletchingley, Godstone, A25, START, Grn, Town Pond, Church Town, A22, Coldharbour Farm, Sandpit, Leigh Place, Tilburstow Common, WALK 30

there is a little quarry hut and a bar across the road, a track will be found running down to the right. Take this and swing left with it along the bottom of a belt of trees, with views over the Weald to the south.

At Coldharbour Farm subsequently reached continue your forward direction for only 50 yards along a tarmac drive. Then, when this latter goes uphill, turn *rightwards* on a firm gravelled track which slopes downhill past a house to a field gate, which can be opened and closed.

Follow this track through the ensuing field to a cottage (seen ahead). In the road reached turn left, uphill. In about 250 yards, or so, where the fields on the right slope up to meet the steep wood-land, a signposted bridleway will be found on the right. It runs along the bottom of the wood and is rather too popular with horseriders. As a consequence it gets much churned up. As an experiment walkers are currently allowed to go along the top edge of the adjacent fields, crossing the fences by stiles (there are no stiles along the woodland bridleway).

After ½ mile a gate gives access to a field across which one cuts diagonally to another field gate from which a track leads down, through woods, to a road. Especially if you have venturesome children or a lively dog racing ahead, be very careful here! This is a section of an old Roman Road and modern horseless chariots cutting a curve of the A22 are very 'busy' on it.

Facing you, inviting your attention, will be a couple of entrances; the rightmost with a bridleway signstone and the other a private drive to Brakey Hill. *Disregard both of these.* Instead, turn left, uphill, for a few yards to a signstoned path on the right. (This currently also carries, on a tree, a sign 'No Horses'.)

Take this, steeply uphill. You are now on Tilburstow (or Tilburstowhill) Common on which, quite frankly, it is difficult to give precise directions as paths are capricious, running through trees and saplings. But you cannot go far astray. If ever in doubt just bear leftwards and you will strike the main road you have not long since quitted. Turn rightwards in this into Godstone.

But if you'd like to be with me, proceed as follows: Follow the steeply rising path, at first veering only slightly rightwards off the main road, being careful not to slide down the left-hand bank. At the top of the hill the track is not well defined. If, here, you go slightly rightwards, downhill, you should find, and follow, a more defined path, still following your initial direction.

At a point on this path where the edge of the trees and a fence protecting a sandpit can be seen about 50 yards to the right, move in that direction. Then turn left, following, generally, the fence. In about 100 yards a valley will be seen on the left, parallel to the line of path. The trees open out a bit and the path runs even more steeply downhill.

Eventually the main road (A22) is reached near a junction of minor roads. The main road *could* be followed leftwards into Godstone but for a more attractive footpath way turn rightwards for about 200 yards to a turning opposite the sandpit entrance (point X).

(Should one bear too sharply rightwards round the sandpit one will find oneself going down a gorse and bramble-covered spine between sandpits. Not to worry! Just keep on to the bottom, crossing a lorry track and descending steps to emerge—again take care!—on the A22. Turn left along the pavement in front of the houses opposite until you come to a turning opposite the sandpit entrance and builders' merchants—point X.)

Either way (from point X) Go along the 'No Through Road' which very soon bends rightwards. Very soon take an enclosed footpath on the left which crosses a dam separating two lakes and goes uphill to join a gravelled track. One notes a purple-painted footpath sign at the entrance to the path, here.

Turn left, following the track round a square right bend to pass the buildings of Leigh Place on the left and, at a square left bend, to a footpath from an iron stile on the right, again with a purple footpath sign.

Follow the uphill, field-edge path, passing in front of a large house and lawn. Subsequently cross a stile on the left. The short enclosed path which ensues brings you to a field in which turn left. In 100 yards a signpost directs you rightwards towards another lake. Cross its dam and climb uphill over a crossing stile into the churchyard of Godstone.

Opposite the churchyard main entrance is a broad tarmac path leading (past the southern end of the Town Pond — a nature reserve) into Godstone village opposite the green, pond and car park.

Turn rightwards with the green on your right, to the north-west corner (where are a café, the Hare and Hounds and toilets). Now take a northward track, between houses, but in only 100 yards get over a stile on the left and enter a small grassy field. Your way is half left of the approach direction but, before continuing, climb the tumulus (ancient burial mound) in front as it gives good views of the North Downs (with the M25 stealing some of the picture).

A stile then gives on to an enclosed path between the sandpits. Maintaining always the same forward direction, subsequently cross a cropped field aiming for a point about 200 yards left of a farm (North Park) seen ahead, reaching a road via a gap. Turn rightwards for about 50 yards to a field gate, which may have to be climbed, on the left.

The way is now diagonally south-west (a *little* more left than squarely left) to another field gate. Beyond this keep the hedge on your right. You then meet a wood and bear left to have the wood on your right. A gap appears on the right from which a bridleway strikes off rightwards to reach a lane (point Y) in a short ¼ mile.

A quick way into Bletchingley is now to turn left in this road, Workhouse Lane, entering the village by the church (used, incidentally by the three denominations: Anglican, Catholic and Methodist). Alternatively, at point Y, one can cross to the road almost opposite. Follow to a T-junction. Here turn left. On reaching a square right bend, continue *forward* on the tarmac path which leads, uphill, to the centre of the village, practically opposite the start.